STRANGERS
in a
FOREIGN LAND

A Testimony of Faith and Endurance

Johan K. McGregor

STRANGERS *in a* FOREIGN LAND

ISBN: 978-1598240733

Printed in the United States of America

ACKNOWLEDGMENTS

In grateful appreciation to our Lord and Savior, Jesus Christ, for the gift of salvation and the beautiful presence of the Holy Spirit. Thank You for the call of God on the lives of my entire family; for the divine visitation in 1956 when my parents' lives were forever changed.

Sincere thanks to my late parents, George and Mary, for teaching their children the ways of the Lord. They have instilled in us not only to love the Lord our God with all our hearts but to pursue His presence.

I want to express my deepest appreciation to my awesome wife, Elize. You are the love of my life. I could not have made this journey without you. You have always stood with me through hardships and trials. Your tireless labor to finalize and oversee the publishing of this book is invaluable.

Special thanks to Manuel and Joeline for running this race with endurance and hanging in there when the going got tough. To Gershon for showing courage and strength as an older brother in some of the most difficult moments on the road.

Thank you to Marie McGregor and Jeanne McGregor for being faithful and diligent in finalizing materials, pictures, and typing manuscripts for this book.

A special thank you to three amazing ladies who labored tirelessly, spending many hours typing, collaborating, and praying over this book. Debra Varossa, Ronda Wehby and Paula Rentfro.

Last but not least, my amazing children: Andrew and Kimi, Raymond, Brandon and Emily, Chantelle and Tim, Justin, Jonathan. I am so proud to be your dad and grateful that God has blessed me with you. Your passion for God is what any parent could only dream of. To my beautiful, sweet, smart, strong, and Jesus-loving grandchildren, Gabriella, Ezra, Judah, Levi, Jeremiah, Elisha Wesley, Shia, and those still to come. Oupa and Oumie love you very much. May this book encourage you to run your race and fulfill the purpose of God in your own generation.

TABLE OF CONTENTS

FOREWORD

Pastor Paul A Baggett - *The Happy Pastor*
Millersville Assembly of God - Nashville, TN

I remember as if it were yesterday, the first time I met the McGregors. There were the two brothers, Manuel and Johan, their wives Joeline and Elize, and their precious children. The children were friendly and polite and greeted me with such respect. The adults were also very gracious and spoke with very charming accents; nevertheless, God helped me to see far beyond those brave smiles and see the pain of rejection and disappointment on their faces. They were a group of people who obviously needed help, and there was a sincerity and honesty about them that let me know we were supposed to help them. Beyond the weary eyes and tired bodies, I discerned an anointing on their lives and a hunger for the things of God.

As I talked with them on the church parking lot that day, I realized that they had been brought up by Godly parents and had been taught to live upright and in the fear of God.

The next morning in the service, as they started singing, the power of God came down in a miraculous way. It was confirmation to me, and we started a revival that day.

After an eight-week revival, I took them on to other revivals with me and introduced them to a few pastor friends of mine. Before long, they were getting invitations from all over the nation, radio stations were playing their music, and they were frequently seen on television.

The ministry of the McGregors has touched, and continues to touch thousands of people around the world. Their music has crossed the barriers of age, culture, race, religion, and denominations. Their vibrant, warm, and friendly personalities have broken down many walls of prejudices and suspicions.

I am very proud of my "sons from afar," as I often refer to them. They have worked very hard, and they are men of prayer. I am proud to be their Pastor, and I still stand ready to help them in any way I can. I thank God for His blessings on them and their ministry.

When I think about the ministry of the McGregors, I am very blessed knowing that the prayers of Reverend George and Mary McGregor are still alive today, as their children carry on with the Gospel of Jesus Christ.

FOREWORD

Pastor John A. Kilpatrick
Senior Pastor
Brownsville Assembly of God - Pensacola, FL

I remember very clearly the day a friend of mine, Pastor C.W. Mullis of Georgia, called me and emphatically pressed upon me to have the McGregors come to Brownsville. I remember him telling me how anointed and talented they were. He emphasized they could not only sing but preach under the anointing. I did not know how providential that call would be. Not only did I invite them to come to Brownsville, but they actually were sent by God for such a time as this. God used this family to prepare the way for revival. When they came, services lasted into the wee hours of the morning. God moved powerfully; as a matter of fact, they were at Brownsville the week prior to the Father's Day Outpouring in 1995.

The McGregors have become my very close friends. They sang at all our Ministers Conferences and have traveled with Steve Hill and me on the road. The McGregors are truly Missionaries from Africa to the U.S.A. As I read the manuscript of each memoir, I was reminded by Holy Spirit just how providential our relationship is.

What a legacy these men have! What a family! What an exciting journey it has been. This is only an interlude - the plot continues - greater things are in store. God always saves the best till last.

FOREWORD

Melba Brendle
Public Relations

Missionaries from Africa to America - It sounds as if somebody got it backward. After all, Americans have sent many missionaries to Africa, and we have all shaken our heads with pity at the pictures of starving and neglected children we support with our prayers and our finances. For many years, America has been faithful to send the Gospel to the Continent of Africa. But could there now be a need for missionaries in America?

We have only to look around us, read the newspaper, or watch the news on television to realize with sadness that we do need a spiritual awakening in our own land. We have fallen far short of the standards and principles we once taught and lived by. Do we need to be reminded of the foundation on which this country was built?

For many years, Americans have been faithful to sow into Africa. Now at a time when we need it most, we reap a harvest. It is a harvest of young, talented, anointed, and dedicated evangelists. They are the sons of a pioneer minister of the Gospel in South Africa, Reverend George Edward McGregor, who was brought to the knowledge of the Full Gospel of Christ by an American missionary. Rev. McGregor's healing crusades throughout South Africa and neighboring countries reached masses of people with the Gospel of Christ in the sixties, seventies, and mid-eighties.

Their testimony is to bear witness to the faithfulness of God. Their trials and triumphs are emotionally expressed as they testify and recall the events and situations that laid the cornerstones for the - now well-known and respected - ministry of the McGregors.

It has been my honor to work with the Ministry of the McGregors for several years. They are some of the most anointed men of God I have ever known. The hardships and heartaches they have faced in this country have only served to make them stronger and more determined to fulfill their calling. I know their hearts and the passion they each possess for the things of God. I have witnessed the evangelistic fire that seems to be 'shut-up in their bones.' I also know their gentle spirits and the love and compassion they have for souls.

I have witnessed the courage and strength of their wives, Elize and Joeline, who understand and share the call of God. It has been a joy to see the bright, happy eyes of their children growing up knowing the love of godly parents. I have seen men and women of integrity bravely follow the call of God and the plan of God for their lives come to fruition.

FOREWORD

Robin Hardin
President of Lebanon Aglow International
Board of Elders, Love's Way Church

Early one Sunday, I received a phone call from one of our church leaders. We were going to vote on the morning's guest speaker, a missionary from South Africa. He was auditioning for the position of Pastor.

My response must have been discouraging. I simply couldn't vote for or against anyone with whom I had only one encounter. At the end of service, Johan McGregor walked down the aisle to exit the sanctuary. I stepped out of my seat, blocking his path. "I don't know about the rest of the people here, but you are my pastor." I have never regretted those words.

Pastor Johan wrote Strangers in a Foreign Land as a testimony of God's grace and provision. If you have ever had to rely on 'duct tape and prayer,' you'll find hope in the miracles he encountered. The mistreatment from fellow Christians caused my heart to grieve. As an American, the prejudice and hostile treatment of others awakened a fresh commitment to the Golden Rule. Strangers in a Foreign Land will inspire you to live life love's way.

1
HELP ME HELP THE PEOPLE

Anna entered the butcher shop carrying a baby in her arms.

Immediately Dad's attention was drawn to the child. The baby's hands, legs, and buttocks looked severely burned.

"What happened to your baby?" he asked as he quickly made his way from behind the counter toward her.

Ashamed, Anna's head dropped as she started to explain in her limited English that both she and her husband work on the farms. "The money we earn is never enough to buy food or any of the other things we need. Instead of worrying, we just spend what little money we have on liquor and drink our cares away. When my husband came home last night, we got drunk. The house was cold, so we made a fire in the center of the room on a metal sheet." (Anna, like so many others, lived in a shack built of scrap boards, pieces of metal and cardboard.)

"We both drank until we passed out." She continued. "Sometime during the night, our baby crawled onto the hot metal sheet, getting these terrible burns and we don't know what to do."

Tears filled Dad's eyes as he took the baby from her and tenderly inspected the wounds. Dad always had a compassionate heart towards the poor, the suffering, and the homeless. He would help them in any way he could. He would often give those in need meat and groceries and pay their rent or electric bills.

Overwhelmed, he cried out to God for His mercy, saying, "If there is a God in heaven, please help me to help these precious people and this poor baby!"

Little did he know that God would hear his desperate cry for help. Soon, God would reveal himself to Dad in a miraculous way that would set the course for an incredible journey of faith.

Rev. George and Mary McGregor

2

A CRY FOR MERCY

My father was a businessman. By the age of 29, he was already running three successful businesses. All the members of the McGregor family were hard-working people. They were known and respected for their honesty, good business ethics, and success.

My parents were married on October 25, 1947. Dad's family was originally from Scotland, and Mom's family was from Portugal. Both were from old traditional churches where the religion was formal and stiff. Their church attendance consisted of special days, Easter and Christmas. Although Dad belonged to the Anglican church, he did not have a personal relationship with God. He only had an awareness of a higher power. Dad's father taught him that if he should ever be in trouble, never forget to pray. So, Dad would occasionally pray.

In the second week of February 1956, in the very early hours of the morning, something dramatic and unusual happened. The hour was late when Dad went to bed for a short night of rest. He had to go to one of his businesses very early the next morning. Dad was still tired when the alarm went off. He said to Mom, "I feel so tired. Let me just close my eyes for maybe twenty or thirty more minutes and then wake me up." Mom set the alarm again and went back to sleep.

Having a butcher's business required Dad to go to the shop very early to prepare meat for the day. The shop had to be open and ready for business at 5:00 a.m. since customers would arrive very early to shop. Dad always worked with such a spirit of excellence. He described himself as a Meat Surgeon, not just a butcher. He always took good care of his customers, always cut their meat to perfection. He wanted his employees and the shop to be clean and presentable. He worked hard to make sure that these things happened.

On this particular morning, he had a very vivid dream. In this dream, he saw himself standing in the butchery wearing a clean white coat and suddenly heard the phone ring. He answered the phone, and a voice said, "Is this George McGregor?" He answered, "Yes." The voice then asked, "Do you have a Bible?" "Yes," Dad replied. "Read Matthew 15:7-9," the voice instructed.

The dream jolted him awake. He quickly woke Mom and said, "Mary, I believe God has spoken to me!" This was no ordinary voice. Dad immediately knew it was the Voice of God.

He got out of bed with his heart racing and hands shaking. Frantically he started looking for his Bible. Because scripture reading was not a regular activity for him, finding his Bible was a challenge. Eventually, he located it and began to read aloud.

"Mary, you've got to hear this! The Bible says, 'Ye hypocrites, well did Isaiah prophesy of you saying, This people draweth nigh unto me with their mouth, and honoureth me with their lips; but their heart is far from me. But in vain they do worship me, teaching for doctrines the commandments of men.'" (KJV)

He read it over and over again until it became real to him. He knew that God was speaking to him when He said, "You're a hypocrite. You honor me with your mouth and your lips, but your heart is far from me."

Early that morning, after realizing God had exposed his heart, Dad fell on his knees and cried out to God, "Oh God, have mercy on me! I'm a sinner, please forgive me. I realize that I have been a hypocrite and I am so sorry. Please come into my heart and change me."

He did not hear someone preach a great sermon, nor was he in a church service somewhere. It happened right in his own bedroom through a dream. God visited our home!

3
PASSION IGNITED

After Dad surrendered his heart to the Lord, life was never the same for our family. This dramatic encounter drastically changed my dad and eventually my mother.

Dad made an appointment with his Anglican priest to tell him what had happened and how his life had changed. The priest just patted him on the back and said, "George, you're a good man. Don't worry too much about it. It was just a dream." However, Dad knew that it was not just an ordinary dream. He knew that this experience had changed his life forever!

Undeterred by the priest's advice, Dad began sharing his testimony with people everywhere; on street corners, buses, trains, and wherever he could find someone to listen.

After Dad's conversion, he could not wait to get home from work, and get ready to go find a house meeting. This became a nightly event. Mom started to get suspicious and accused him of having another lover.

One evening as Dad got ready to leave, Mom sat in his car waiting. When Dad got in the car she said, "Ok, take me to where you 'say' you are going every night." Dad drove to the house where the meetings were held. Several people were already waiting for the service to begin. The man of the house asked Dad to minister and share his testimony. After speaking, Dad gave the altar call. Guess who stood up, walked forward and surrendered her life to Jesus? My precious mother! She too found the lover of her soul.

Mom suffered for years with painful ingrown toenails. Many visits to the doctor yielded no solution to her problem. A man of God, Brother Pedro from the country of Angola came to our home. He was known for walking down the streets, praying in Portuguese. Children would line up to have a blessing spoken over them. He would declare, "Em nome do Pai e do Filho e do Santo Espírito!" as he waved his hands over the children's heads. (In the name of the Father and of the Son and the Holy Spirit.) Brother Pedro prayed for Mom, pouring water on her feet. The pain left immediately and she was totally healed from her condition from that day forward.

Even though Dad was busy ministering, he still had a business to run. He had a big family to support but found himself losing interest in the butcher shops. One day, a well-known prophet, Brother John Bentum, came to see my dad. Brother Bentum began to prophesy and said to Dad. "The

Lord wants you to fully trust Him and go full time into the ministry and preach the gospel to the Nations!"

Dad had been actively ministering in cottage meetings, local churches, and community centers.
Dad didn't think, with a wife, six boys, and one girl, that would be possible. He worked all day, ministered in the evenings and weekends, and felt like that was enough. As time passed, Dad lost everything. He lost his business, his two-story house, and his cars. He had to move his family in with his brother, Davie and his wife, Nenna.

After Dad was saved, he developed a deep hunger for prayer. It became his lifestyle. Whenever we left the house to go anywhere, we would always pray.

One night in particular, in the early fall of 1959, the family was going to hear a Jewish evangelist, Hymie Rubinstein, who was ministering in the area. Everyone was dressed and ready to leave and, naturally, went to the living room to pray. Dad began to pray. His prayer just went on and on and on. It seemed like it went on forever. The younger children were getting restless, so Mom asked George, the oldest of the children, to take them to the kitchen and make them a sandwich.

There was a door that separated the living room and the kitchen. As everyone exited the living room, they could hear Dad praying. Suddenly, his language changed, and Dad started speaking in an unknown language that they had never heard him speak before.

Inquisitively, George opened the door and peeked through. It was definitely still Dad praying. He was on his knees, and he was the one speaking this foreign language.

As George observed, it looked like his mouth was on fire. Gershon and Owen stood with George, peeking through the door. Dad was praying in tongues. He prayed in tongues for hours and hours and many days after that.

Even at his new job managing a butcher shop, he continued speaking in tongues. A man of Arab descent, a Muslim, came into the business, heard Dad speaking in tongues, and ran out of the building. He came back a few moments later, saying, "I never knew you could speak my language. I heard you say, 'The name of the Lord must be praised! The name of the Lord must be praised!'"

Dad had been gloriously filled with the Holy Spirit according to Acts 1:8.

One morning at about 2:00 a.m., the Holy Spirit convicted Dad of a time when he took R10 (ten rand) from a cash register. He intended to pay it back but never did. He was much younger when he managed a butcher shop for a man named Mr. Wallach. Dad immediately got out of bed, dressed, and drove 50 miles to the man's house. When he arrived, he knocked on the door of the two-story home. The man opened the door and said, "McGregor, what is wrong? What are you doing here?!" Dad confessed about the money he took many years ago and told him he was there to pay it back.

Frustrated, Mr. Wallach replied, "I am sleeping! Could you not have waited until tomorrow when the sun came up?" "No," Dad said. Dad explained that he had recently gotten saved, and God had changed his life. He needed to make things right.

When God filled my dad with the Holy Spirit, He began preparing him for ministry and a life of holiness and obedience. God again sent this prophet to tell Dad to go into the ministry full-time. Three times God spoke through Brother Bentum, but he would not heed the call. The prophet told him, because of his disobedience, he would be involved in an automobile accident. He told Dad that no one would die as a result of the accident.

Then it happened. One night after a cottage meeting, Mom and Dad were going to drop a friend at her house on their way home. At this time, Mom was seven months pregnant with me. They were talking about the service as Dad drove. He turned his head to say something to the lady sitting in the backseat when Mom suddenly shouted, "George! Look out!"

A big dump truck had stopped in the road in front of them. Their car slammed right into the rear of the truck. Mom's head went through the windshield, cutting her face from the corner of her mouth to her ear. The steering wheel broke as it smashed into Dad's chest, crushing several ribs. He also suffered a broken nose.

The doctors were unable to stop the bleeding from Mom's injury. Dad simply laid his hands on her wound, and the bleeding stopped immediately. Amazingly, while they were treated at the hospital for their own injuries, Dad walked around laying hands on other patients, praying for them to be healed as well.

While Dad was recovering from his injuries and unable to work, God miraculously provided our every need. One morning, Brother Bentum and two of his friends came over to visit. Dad was still in much pain from his chest injury, so he asked Brother Bentum to pray for him. He laid his hands on Dad's chest and prayed a short prayer. Dad said Brother

Bentum's hands felt like a hot iron, and when he removed his hands, all his pain was gone. After experiencing God's healing power for the first time for himself, Dad asked God to give him the gift of healing and miracles. Now a passion was ignited in him to take the gospel to people everywhere.

4
LEARNING OBEDIENCE

For the next few months, Dad was in training, learning to hear and obey the voice of the Holy Spirit. Some of the things he did seemed crazy and foolish. Even Mom started to get worried, however later came to understand and trust the voice of the Holy Spirit.

Early one morning, Dad got dressed in his suit and bow tie. He told Mom he needed to go to the city of Cape Town. With his Bible under his arm, he traveled by bus and then by train. Upon his arrival at Central Station in Cape Town, Dad looked around, unsure what he was to do next. God then directed him to cross the street and go to a jewelry store. As he looked through the window at the different watches, he heard the Lord say to look closer at a particular one and read the brand name, "STAYRITE!" The Lord then told him, "Now you can go back home." That was it; God only wanted to test his obedience and have him receive the message in the name of a watch, "Stay right!"

On another occasion, Dad took George with him to the city of Cape Town. As they walked, they crossed a busy street. Suddenly Dad stopped in the middle of the road, removed his hat, and knelt on one knee to pray. Then he got up and continued on his way. I can only imagine what was going through George's mind as a teenager.

After supper one evening, the family was all sitting around the kitchen table talking about the Lord. All of a sudden, Dad stood up, walked over to the woodstove, opened the door, and stuck his hands in the fire. They could not believe what they were seeing, but to everyone's shock, Dad's hands did not burn.

Another time, Dad got out of bed in the middle of the night and went to the bathroom. After some time, Mom went to check on him. To her surprise, she found him sitting in a tub of cold water, in his pajamas, praying. Shaken, Mom ran to wake up George, Gershon, and Owen. Through her tears, she declared, "It must be true what the people are saying about your dad; he's crazy, he's lost his mind."

Shortly after, Dad got dressed and went to the living room to pray. He then called Mom and the children into the living room and told them that while he was praying, he heard the Lord speaking to him, saying, "Thank you, thank you for being obedient like an Abraham." He then continued to explain that the Lord had been testing him for the past few months to see if he would be obedient to the voice of the Holy Spirit. This ability to discern God's Voice, and to respond with unquestioning obedience, would prove to be a key aspect of the ministry that the Lord had planned for George McGregor.

"Walk in obedience to all that the Lord your God has commanded you, so that you may live and prosper and prolong your days in the land that you will possess."
Deuteronomy 5:33 (NIV)

"And all these blessings shall come upon you and overtake you, because you obey the voice of the Lord your God."
Deuteronomy 28:2 (NKJV)

5

EXPERIENCING HIS PRESENCE

Dad had been saved for about three years when he began to hold what was referred to as Cottage Meetings in our home. Many people would come to pray and seek the face of God through the night until early morning. Dad would also hold meetings where they would "tarry" for the baptism of the Holy Spirit. People would come to our house, especially on Friday evenings. They would pray through the night until daybreak. Many people would be filled with the Holy Spirit.

Word spread of the miracles and how God was moving in those meetings. People came from all over to hear Dad's miraculous testimony and to witness the power of God in action! Dad's John the Baptist style of preaching and his uncompromising delivery of the Gospel made him the subject of much ridicule and persecution.

Established churches did not always welcome him, so he would drive around to find wherever people gathered and ministered to them there. He then began holding open-air meetings, and after praying for a tent for ten years, finally conducted large tent crusades.

Dad continued to develop a deep hunger and thirst for the things of God. Just as Jesus would go away alone to spend time with His Father, so was the practice of my father. Dad and three of his closest friends would travel to Table Mountain in Cape Town on many occasions. They would often spend the entire weekend there fasting, praying, seeking, and experiencing the presence of God.

During the crusades, Dad would make a daily announcement calling the people to meet him at 5:00 a.m. at the top of the nearest mountain or hill for special prayer. Many people, hungry for God, would show up for these early morning prayer meetings. They would stay and pray for several hours. As a young boy, I still remember the people singing and rejoicing as they returned with Dad from these prayer meetings. They would march straight into the big tent, fired up with the power of God, ready for the 10:00 a.m. service. The powerful impact of God's presence was astounding!

In the beautiful city of Cape Town, there is a popular outdoor marketplace called The Grand Parade, simply referred to as The Parade. It was always very busy, especially on Wednesdays and Saturdays. Vendors selling their wares, shoppers, and those gathered just to socialize, crowded the area. With its monuments, large statues, and stone steps, The Parade made the perfect amphitheater setting. You could also always count on a pigeon or two to find their perch on the heads of the dignified statues. Often speakers would stand on the tall steps or at the base of a statue to speak or preach to the people.

When we were still very young, Dad started going to The Parade on Saturdays to hold services. We ran electrical cords to a small generator and hooked up our musical instruments and microphones. George played the guitar, and either Gershon or Manuel played the accordion. George had a unique and powerful singing voice. His rich, soulful tones, along with the energetic music that filled the air, would quickly draw the attention of the people milling around the busy area. Within a few minutes, a large crowd would gather around. That is when Dad would step up, take the microphone and start preaching. We would see fantastic miracles happen right before our eyes! There were wonderful healings and hundreds and hundreds of salvations.

Even today, the people of Cape Town remember those services and talk about the miraculous things that happened. Anytime we visit that area, many people still recognize the McGregors. They tell us how they remember the wonderful times, songs of praise, and the powerful preaching of the Word. Most importantly, they share how God forever changed their lives and the lives of their families - all because of a man who followed the call of God to preach the Gospel of Jesus Christ!

Because of Dad's sincere desire for everyone to hear the message of hope and healing found in Jesus Christ, God began expanding his ministry. In the years to come, George and Mary McGregor would establish a great nationwide ministry in our homeland of South Africa.

The Parade Cape Town, South Africa.
Crowds gathering to hear the Gospel as Dad ministers.
George singing and playing guitar, Manuel playing the accordion.

6

RACIAL DIVIDE

In the early days of Dad's crusades (1960-the 70s), South Africa's apartheid laws required that he span a rope down the middle of the tent to separate the whites and the blacks. However, Dad refused to adhere to this ungodly, ridiculous practice of discrimination. He believed that God created all people in His image and of the same blood, therefore, we should love everyone. People of all races came to Dad's crusade meetings. As word spread about the mixed services, it caused problems with the local government.

In the early 1960s, Dad held a crusade in a small town called Montague in the western province. Many people were saved and wanted to be baptized. Because the team was leaving early the next morning for another crusade, the only time Dad was available to baptize was at 4:00 a.m. The news started to spread that the crazy evangelist, George McGregor, was going to baptize people in the Kings River on the outskirts of town. As the day was breaking, hundreds of people began filling the streets, walking toward the river. Many were standing on the bridge, and others gathered on the grassy banks, singing the praises of God. More than one hundred people were going to be baptized that early morning.

There was a white Afrikaans speaking lady who accepted Christ during this crusade and also wanted to be baptized in the Kings River. However, her pastor from the Dutch Reformed Church, adamantly opposed it.
"Over my dead body will you be baptized with those black people!" he exclaimed. Ignoring his threats, she chose to be baptized with her black brothers and sisters.

Undercover police officers were sent to the meetings on several occasions. When Dad spotted them, he would direct the audience to sing the National Anthem of South Africa. Almost immediately, these men would jump to attention. Then Dad would ask all the people to stand and welcome our friends from the government. "Here's one, there's one, and oh, there's another!" With their cover blown, the undercover officials would just turn and walk out — what a clever way of handling a potential disruption. As the services continued, God's presence would fill the tent, resulting in hundreds of people getting saved and many healed. The most beautiful sight to see was people of all races lying side by side on the sawdust floor, touched by the power of God.

In those days, many prominent church leaders, pastors, and evangelists were very prejudiced against anyone whose skin tone was not as white as theirs - especially against those of non-white ethnic origin or black people. Some of Dad's preacher friends even told him, "You spend too much time in the black locations. There's no money there!"

A famous evangelist once told Dad, "Brother McGregor, I don't know why you waste your time preaching to the black man. He does not even have a soul." Shocked at this statement, Dad immediately rebuked him, telling him to repent and ask God for forgiveness. Just a few years later, this man began using drugs and alcohol and lost his ministry. In a continuous effort to restore him, Dad would go out looking for him, usually finding him in a bar or hotel room. Dad would pick him up and bring him to our house. He could be heard praying and crying in his room. Later, he would tell Dad, "I don't feel God anymore... I don't feel God anymore...." This man's spiritual condition broke Dad's heart.

Many well-known American evangelists and missionaries came to South Africa and neighboring countries holding vast crusades. Because they felt the people were too poor to give, they did not teach them the principles of tithes and offerings. Dad encouraged giving to the Lord as the Word of God teaches and was criticized severely for receiving free will offerings in his meetings. He taught that if the principle of giving and receiving works for one group of people, the same truth must and will work for any group of people. Failing to teach this would keep the people poor and in bondage. He sincerely believed that God could break the curse of poverty and pour out blessings on their lives.

Dad held revival meetings near Upington at the Augrabies Water Falls, about five hundred miles west of Johannesburg. Racial prejudices were very strong in this area. One day, Gershon, George, and some of our team members went to buy food at a local convenience store. The clerk refused to serve them and called for the owner of the shop. When the owner came, he rudely told them to get out. He shouted, "Blacks are to use the side doors to be served!"

George was not going to stand idly by and allow this man to insult our friends. He told the shop owner, "These men already have the goods in their hands. All you have to do is take their money." But the shop owner refused and demanded that they get out and go to the side door. "They are not leaving until you have served them!" George said sternly. Nevertheless, they were shoved out the door; tempers flared, and a scuffle broke out. It's not hard to imagine how badly this situation could have ended if not for Gershon's intervening with a voice of reason to calm everyone down. Unfortunately, this type of discrimination toward those with a different skin color was the norm at the time.

In 1983, we held a crusade in a black township in Delmas, about two hours northeast of Johannesburg. These meetings ran for a few weeks.

On one particular day, Dad the ministry team was a few miles from the big tent. They were stopped by a large group of policemen in armored military vehicles, forcing them to pull off to the side of the road. The date was March 12th, Dad's birthday. Without much explanation, the entire team was arrested and taken to the local police station. There they learned they were charged for not having written permission from the local government to enter a black location, and certainly not allowed to hold a healing crusade in that area! Dad was threatened by an aggressive police captain who waved his fist and weapon in Dad's face. Showing incredible restraint, Dad reminded the police officer that he was speaking to a man of God. He also told him that God would deal with him if he did not repent and allow the crusade to continue. Shortly after they were arrested, the team was able to present the official paperwork proving that the crusade director had obtained the necessary permission several weeks prior. The charges were dropped. Thankfully, Dad and the team did not spend the night in jail.

A few months later, we learned this police captain had been arrested for stealing truckloads of food supplies and selling them on the black market and also getting a big cut from the local beer halls.

Despite racial prejudice and many attempts to stop him, Dad persevered and continued to hold tent crusades as well as open-air meetings throughout South Africa.

Crusades during the early ministry of
Rev. George McGregor

7

Signs, Wonders, Miracles

And these signs will follow those who believe:
In My name they will cast out demons; they will speak with
new tongues; they will take up serpents; and if they drink
anything deadly, it will by no means hurt them; they will lay
hands on the sick, and they will recover.
Mark 16:17-20 NKJV

Dad's ministry was marked by signs, wonders, and miracles.

The lame walked, the blind saw, the dumb spoke, the deaf heard, the barren received children, and the dead were raised. Many were delivered from demonic possession and oppression.

Paarl - 1964

The first of large Open-Air Crusades

Pastor Maralack, a prominent church leader in the community, became a mighty blessing and influence in Dad's ministry. He organized Dad's first large open-air crusade in Paarl. Without realizing it, the crusade was planned during the heavy rain season. The first night, thick clouds began to form in the distance. Despite the thunder and lightning, the people continued to gather. As the rain began to fall, the people did not leave. Dad's heart was moved because the people were so desperate to hear the Word of God. He stretched out his hands to heaven and prayed a simple prayer, "Lord, Your people have come to hear Your Word tonight on this open field. Let the rain stop only until the service has ended. In Jesus Name, Amen."

Pastor Maralack shared that after Dad prayed, suddenly, the clouds moved around the entire area. For the duration of the service, not a drop of rain fell. The meeting continued, and many people received Jesus as their Savior.

Miracles of supernatural healings were reported. A teenager, who was blind from birth, received her sight! There was a local woman who had been crippled for many years. Her hands, wrists, and arms were curled and drawn to her chest, and she had difficulty walking. She was unable to cook, clean, or care for herself. That night, she was completely healed. She started walking, raising her hands, moving her fingers, shouting, "I'm healed! I'm healed! I'm healed!" The Paarl Revival of 1964 launched Dad's ministry to even larger crusades throughout South Africa.

Athlone - Mid 1960s

On a large open field in Athlone, many people came to hear the Word of God. Athlone is a suburb of Cape Town located to the east of the City Center on the Cape Flats. This area was well known for its gang violence. During the service, a car came and parked near the stage area. Three men in the car began smoking marijuana. They began laughing loudly, mocking and blowing their smoke in the direction of the people. Dad asked the men not to blow their smoke toward the people and to be respectful while the service was going on. However, they refused and continued their irreverent behavior disrupting the whole service. After several requests for these men to stop, Dad rebuked them, saying, "Because you have disrespected the work of God and would not listen, God will deal with you." Later, we heard that these three men, returning home from work, jumped on the back of an open bus. The bus took a sharp turn, smashed into a wall, crushing and killing all three men.

Free State - Mid 1960s

Apostle Daniel Hofmeister, a longtime friend of the family, was a new convert when he began attending the crusades. He was an eyewitness to many miracles and how God used Dad in an unusual way. Daniel recounts, "I saw all the nine gifts of the Holy Spirit operating in your dad's ministry. The gift of healing and the working of miracles was especially dominant. I was there during the Free State Crusade when a crippled beggar leaped to his feet and started walking as the power of God hit him. The passion and zeal that your dad had for the Lord left an impression upon my life."

Daniel and his wife, Julia (my cousin), later started to travel with the team on many crusades all across South Africa. They witnessed firsthand the supernatural power of the Holy Spirit operating in the meetings. "I saw many souls come to know the Lord and were baptized in water. I am forever grateful to God for linking me with your dad, a man who played a significant role in my formative years in ministry. I believe that some of that anointing rubbed off on me as we ministered together for the Lord." he shared. Daniel eventually founded a vibrant church called Christ the Life in Cape Town, South Africa. Praise the Lord!

Worcester - The Early 1970s
One testimony of healing was of a seven-year-old boy who was crippled since birth. He could not walk and would be left to the mercy of others to carry him. Dad prayed for the boy and felt that God had healed him. They took the boy home, still crippled and unable to walk. The crusade had ended, and a few weeks had passed when a letter arrived in the mail.

The letter was from the parents of the boy, testifying of what had happened. The letter explained that every morning the mother carried the child outside. She placed him on a mat to enjoy the sun and to watch the other children play. One morning from her kitchen window, she saw him suddenly jump to his feet and start running after the other children. Praise God! Their son was completely healed by the power of God!

A tribal woman came for prayer during a morning service. On her leg was a big open sore that would not heal. Dad prayed over a jug of water and told the woman to wash her leg while pouring the water over the sore. That night, Dad had a dream of a big spider coming out of a woman's leg. The next day, this woman came back holding a glass container with something in it that looked like a spider. She testified that when she washed her leg that night, this thing came out with roots and all. This was another miracle - Glory to God!

During many of our tent revivals, we could hear drums beating throughout the night. It was the sangomas (witch doctors) who were calling up evil spirits to stop and disrupt the preaching of the gospel of Jesus Christ. One night after one of the services had ended and the people had gone home, Dad heard the drums beating and felt the presence of evil and smelled a foul odor all around the tent. He gathered all the team members and began praying and rebuking the enemy and the devil's strongholds over that region. Many people were gloriously saved and set free by the power of the Holy Spirit during those meetings.

On another occasion, a woman came running into a morning service, requesting immediate prayer for her daughter and two-year-old grandbaby. She just heard that they had been in a terrible accident. Their car had flipped several times, and the baby had been thrown out. Dad immediately joined hands with this grandmother, and while praying, he had a vision of little bones being mended and healed. After prayer, Dad told the lady that the baby would be alright and that she would have no broken bones whatsoever. Good news came the same day that the child had no broken bones, and both mother and child were released from the hospital with only minor scrapes and bruises.

Windhoek - Mid 1970s
Namibia, on the west coast of Africa

During an open-air crusade in Windhoek, hundreds of people gave their hearts to the Lord. While many were kneeling, with tears running down their faces, a man tossed a dead snake among them, disrupting the service. People jumped up and began screaming and running in every direction. Dad tried to calm the people down to continue the service. He urged the person responsible for throwing the snake to come forward and repent, declaring that if he would, then God would forgive him. However, no one came forward. Dad then began to prophesy that whoever did this would run naked through the streets. Several weeks later, news came that a man suffered a mental breakdown and then ran naked through the streets, with his family members trying to catch him.

Crusades near Johannesburg - 1977
Natalspruit

A woman, who we all learned to know as Ouma (which means Grandma), heard about the tent crusade in Natalspruit. She asked someone to take her there as she was too weak to walk without support. Her feet were always swollen, her kidneys ached, and she had high blood pressure. Her eyesight was so bad that she had to wear extra thick glasses. Ouma shared with us that when she came near the tent and heard the singing, she suddenly began to feel stronger. By the time she entered the tent, she was able to walk without help. She was completely healed that night. Now she could walk, run, and care for herself. Her life was miraculously changed forever.

Ouma became my mother's best friend. She was an excellent cook and loved to help my mother around the house. She became a cherished member of our family. Ouma began to help with the crusades by cooking food for the workers and anyone hungry. As the tent was being raised, she would also gather the other women to pray and intercede for the meetings.

The miracle Ouma received impacted her whole family. I can still see her daughter, Joyce, faithfully bringing people in her pickup truck to the crusades, long after her mother passed. These are precious memories; great is her reward!

Germiston - 1977

In October, Waiter Ntunja came to the crusade a desperate man. He was very sick with undiagnosed disease, and his whole body was in constant pain. He had consulted with witch doctors and prayed to his ancestors, but they were unable to cure him. George was preaching that night. Mr. Ntunja remembered George saying that the Holy Spirit cannot live together with smoking and drinking, and you must stop. He continued to share, "His words sounded so personal to me. My heart was pricked so much that I surrendered my life to Jesus that day. I was totally set free from my addictions, and I kept attending the crusade. I quit my secular job in 1979 to become part of the crusade team. I was responsible for tent pitching and security. Over the years, I saw thousands of people delivered from demon possession and many different kinds of sicknesses. I am now a pastor, and I have learned the virtues of love, truth, boldness, integrity, and prayerfulness from Father McGregor, the man of God." Waiter has been with the ministry for over forty years. He is currently serving as an outreach pastor at Mt. Calvary Pentecostal Church with Bishop Owen McGregor.

Thembisa - 1978

Anastina Seemela testified, "My life was empty and troubled when the tent Crusade came to Thembisa in February 1978. At that time, Pastor McGregor was overseas, and his son, Owen McGregor, was preaching in his place. I saw blind people receive their sight and the crippled walk. I had never seen anything like this before." Anastina was still not ready to surrender her life to Christ. A few weeks later, while Anastina was attending a three-day conference at the McGregor farm in Midrand, Dad gave a word of knowledge. "There is a woman here who has a growth in her womb," he said. "You are 38 years old, and God wants to heal you." That woman turned out to be Anastina's neighbor. She responded and came forward for prayer. Two days later, a ball-like mass came out of her body. She was miraculously healed! Anastina could no longer deny the power of God! "This made me believe, and I surrendered my life to Jesus," she told us. Anastina began to follow Dad's ministry and later became one of the singers and interpreters for his crusades. Currently, she is serving as one of the pastors at Mt. Calvary Pentecostal Church in Johannesburg.

Randfontein - 1978

We held a tent crusade in Randfontein in 1978, about an hour from Johannesburg. The tent was packed with people ready to receive something from the Lord. Owen was preaching that night when he noticed a commotion toward the entrance of the tent. A woman, crying uncontrollably, held a dead baby wrapped in a blanket. She explained this was her grandchild and her husband came home drunk, demanding food. She told him there was no food since he did not bring home any money. In his terrible rage, he grabbed the crying baby from her arms and threw the child on the cement floor. The baby stopped crying and stopped breathing. Panicking, she remembered advertisements about a tent in the area where the man of God prayed for sick people. She took the child in her arms and ran to the tent, hoping they could pray for her grandbaby. My brother Owen took the child in his arms and asked all the people to believe with him that God would bring life back to this baby. As he prayed, he felt the baby kick and heard crying. God breathed His breath into this precious baby. Owen later said, "It was the most beautiful cry of any baby I had ever heard." To God be the Glory.

Also in Randfontein, a well-respected man in his community came requesting prayer. Ernest and Rebecca Dhlamini could not have children. As a result of this, his family pressured him to leave his wife, blaming her for not giving him children. Dad laid hands on them and asked God to bless them with a child. One year later, God gave them a sweet baby girl named Blessing! To God be all the glory. Today Ernest and Rebecca Dhlamini have four beautiful children. This couple later became pastors of a branch of Mt. Calvary Pentecostal Church in the village of Mohlakeng, just outside the city of Randfontein, South Africa.

"He sent his Word and healed them,
and delivered them from their destruction."
Psalm 107:20 (NKJV)

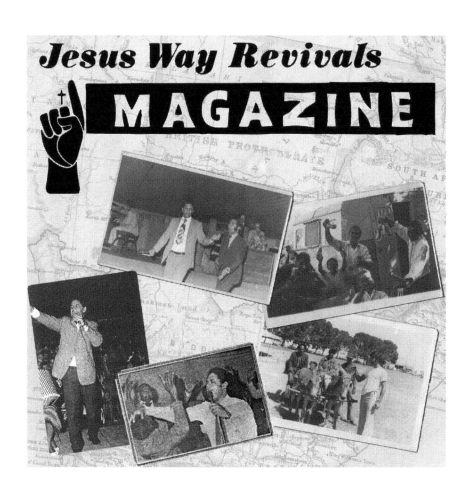

8

BLAZING A GOSPEL TRAIL

The ministry grew as Dad blazed a gospel trail throughout South Africa and neighboring countries. I remember Reinhardt Bonnke, then just a young evangelist from Germany, setting up his big ten-thousand-seat tent on one side of Soweto while we set up our tent on the other side. This area was a few miles outside of the city of Johannesburg. Both ministries were reaching precious souls for the Kingdom of God and seeing mighty miracles in these crusades. Evangelist Bonnke outgrew his tent and started meeting on large open fields with hundreds of thousands of people attending.

For more than thirty years, Dad preached the Gospel of Jesus Christ and pioneered many churches throughout South Africa. God's bountiful blessings remained on our family. We learned to play various musical instruments at a very young age, singing together with family harmony.

When I was only four years old, Dad would place me on a box or chair and tell me to sing to the people. I remember singing an Afrikaans song, "Hy wys my sy hande deurboor vir my sonde". (He showed me his hands, pierced for my sins.)

My sister, Rosalind, vividly remembers people being healed while hearing the words of this song.

Another time, I vaguely remember sitting between Mom and Dad on the armrest of our car as we were traveling home after a meeting. We were lost deep in an unsafe area of a township. I heard a voice directing me to tell Dad, "Turn here, go to the next road and turn." The Lord led us safely back to our home.

When George was about seventeen years old, he joined Dad full-time in the ministry. At school, he suffered much persecution because Dad was a Pentecostal preacher. Dad quickly became known and ridiculed throughout the community for his unorthodox ministry style, witnessing on street corners and public transportation. Many times, after school, George was mocked, beat up, and spat upon. As a result, he reached the point where he decided to leave school and join Dad as the worship leader and interpreter in the ministry. In Dad's absence, he would also preach.

A couple of years later, Gershon also decided to join the ministry full time. George and Gershon would do event planning and preparation. On one particular morning, they were leading the prayer service while Dad was away on business. A family had traveled at least fifty miles in a donkey cart. Their frail donkey was so thin that you could count every rib. They were bringing their son, who was in thin pajamas and covered with a burlap sack. He was suffering from tuberculosis and in great pain. They had come looking for the man of God. George told them that Rev. McGregor was not there and was about to send them away. Seeing the disappointment on their faces, compassion rose in him, and he remembered what Dad would do. George felt that they could not just send them away but must pray for their son. He asked Gershon to get some oil. They anointed him and prayed a simple, straightforward prayer, rebuking the sickness from the young man's body in the name of Jesus.

Feeling the need to feed them, Gershon left to get them something to eat. George watched as the young man got off the back of the cart, stood to his feet, and began to walk as strength returned to his body! Praise God!

This experience marked the beginning of their own ministries, preaching the glorious gospel of Jesus Christ with signs, wonders, and miracles following.

After graduation, Owen went to university to become a doctor. He was determined not to become part of the ministry. He did not want to have the financial struggle and be the object of ridicule. Over the next few years, God began to transform his life powerfully. He fell deeply in love with Jesus and surrendered to the call to preach the gospel. God literally changed the trajectory of his life. Owen joined the ministry and began preaching full-time. Dad began to send him out to hold crusades in many cities and villages all over South Africa, Namibia, and parts of Zambia.

Our sister, Rosalind, took care of the younger boys - Gregg, Manuel, Roy, and myself - while Mom and Dad traveled with the ministry. When the younger brothers were in school, Rosalind worked in Cape Town. She would use her earnings to buy our school clothes and groceries. Later, she became Dad's secretary. Writing letters to the city officials to get permits for the crusades was her responsibility. She also edited our monthly ministry magazine.

When Gregg, Manuel, Roy, and myself were in high school, the principal would have us sing in the Monday morning assembly. He would share a devotional and pray, and then we would sing gospel songs. We were also invited to go to different singing events. We were known as the *Gospel Lights*. On our school breaks, we would travel and sing at the crusades.

Mom and Dad had faithfully prayed for God to anoint each one of us in a special way. Dad always encouraged us to sing, play music, and write our own songs. Anointed Praise and Worship played an important role throughout Dad's years of ministry. We all became very active in the crusades, playing instruments, special singing, youth ministries, as well as advertising, and of course, it was also our job to set up and take down those big tents.

Not only were all my siblings serving in ministry, but as time progressed, our spouses would eventually be involved in the ministry as well. We formed a group called *The One Way Band* and later changed the name to *Jericho*. We traveled and performed in many gospel singing events and became well known all over South Africa.

9
STRANGE THINGS

After several years of ministry, our family moved to Paarl. We had been living in Cape Town, but Dad's ministry had expanded to Paarl and the surrounding areas. He felt it was necessary to move closer to where the revivals were happening.

I was about three years old when we moved to the big, beautiful farmhouse. However, as time passed, strange things began to happen. One night, Mom sent Manuel to our bedroom to get something. He did not want to go down the hallway. Mom finally persuaded him to tell her why. He told her he was afraid of the little man standing at the end of the hallway watching him. Another night, all of us boys were in our bedroom. Mom came in, long after everyone was asleep, and found me climbing onto the windowsill. I was trying to pry the window open, and no one knew why. She gently put me back in bed and prayed over us.

Another time, Mom thought she heard Dad coming up the driveway in a large truck. She could hear what sounded like chains dragging behind the truck. When she looked outside, she saw no one.

On different occasions, doors would open and close on their own. Sometimes, when we walked into certain areas of the house, we would sense an evil presence, and our hair would stand on end.

Strange things were happening. We were told the revival meetings stirred up different factions of witchcraft. So many were being set free from demonic oppression and possession, and obviously, this had upset the enemy.

One night while Dad was away, we were sitting at the kitchen table after dinner. Suddenly, we heard a loud pelting noise on the metal roof. We were startled because it was so loud. Wondering if it could be raining or hailing, we rushed to the doors and windows to see what it was. It was not raining, and there was no sign of hail on the ground, so we ran out on the front porch. We only saw darkness, bushes, and trees. The loud noise had only lasted a short while and went away as quickly as it came. This was very strange.

The next night around the same time, it happened again. Now we were even more afraid. We thought it might be someone upset with Dad, hiding in the tree line and throwing rocks. Gershon, Owen, and Gregg grabbed cricket bats and ran outside, looking for whoever was doing this. They returned after finding no one. The next night we were determined to solve the mystery. We spanned a length of twine from tree to tree, thinking maybe this would trip them, and we would catch the culprits. Late the next evening, it happened again, yet we saw no one.

This continued night after night while Dad was away. Mom decided to call the police. Two officers arrived in a Land Rover and came into the house to fill out a report. They reassured Mom that everything would be alright and not to worry. While they were there, it happened again! One of the police officers was spooked, and he let out a big ugly curse word. He told Mom that they would be back as they rushed to their vehicle and took off, obviously scared to death. Now, we were really afraid.

That night, when Dad arrived home, we ran outside to meet him, telling him everything that happened. He looked around the outside of the house for any evidence but found nothing. He immediately gathered us together to pray. It was clear to Dad that this was demonic activity, and he was fed up with it.

He told George and Gershon to set up the equipment on the front porch. We set up the speakers, plugged in the guitar and microphone. Dad told George to sing songs about the blood of Jesus. It was about 1:00 a.m.

While George was singing, Dad told the rest of us to run around the outside perimeter of the house and sing along. We ran and sang *"There is power, power, wonder-working power, in the blood of the Lamb."* We could hear Dad praying and George playing the guitar and singing. Apparently, so could all the neighbors because we noticed them coming out of their houses. They stood wrapped in blankets, watching us running, singing, and clapping our hands. We couldn't help but wonder what they were thinking. They were accustomed to Dad holding meetings on the property, just not in the wee hours of the morning.

We had just completed one of our laps around the house when Dad took the microphone and began to pray. Our neighbors had gathered closer, listening intently, as he rebuked the demonic activity. With his hand stretched out, he commanded that devil to stop in the Name of Jesus! Declaring, "the Blood of Jesus is against you, satan. You will not continue this attack!" Dad had prayed other nights, but this night was with different authority. That was the last demonic activity to occur in our home.

I have many fond memories of our time at the old farmhouse. Dad made our home a house of prayer. I remember Dad calling us to pray by loudly clapping his hands. Whether we were playing outside, doing homework, or any other activity, we would immediately stop to go pray.

One thing that always stayed with me and still brings fond memories is when Mom and Dad prayed at night in their room. Us kids could hear them through the wall. Dad would mention each one of us by name, from the oldest to the youngest. He started with George..., then Gershon..., then Owen..., then Rosalind... I knew it would be a long time before he would get to me, being the youngest of eight. I kept listening with my ear against the wall as he would go down the list of names until my name was mentioned. Then I listened intently to the prayer he prayed over me and then finally dozed off.

After living there for several years, our family moved. We were delighted to learn that the city of Paarl bought the property and made it an assisted living home, appropriately naming it House of Grace.

10

MACHETES ON THE ALTAR

Having crusade meetings did not come without risk. We often ministered in very dangerous areas. Dad would always pray and follow the leading of the Holy Spirit as to the location for each crusade, despite police warnings. Gangs would show up to fight right outside the tent. Security was necessary, and to ensure the safety of the people coming to the service, my brothers and I were both the worship team and security team.

One night, Gregg was greeting the people before service when a man pulled out a butcher knife and tried to stab him in the head. He quickly dodged, avoiding a fatal blow. On another occasion, Gregg was struck on the forehead with a huge, heavy pipe wrench while trying to calm down an angry man. He needed several stitches. Once, a man came from the shadows and threw a rock the size of a soccer ball, hitting Manuel on the head, knocking him to the ground. I also recall the night a young gang member started slashing the tent canvas and tie-down ropes. We were able to stop him before he could cut enough ropes to bring the tent down.

One morning at 3:00 a.m., Dad and Gershon were awakened by several gang members pounding on the camper door, screaming demands. The rest of us were sleeping in the tent. While Dad was talking to the gang, Gershon slipped away and woke us up. In the dark tent, we scrambled to get dressed, grabbed the nearest tent side poles, ran toward the gang, and chased them off. As they ran away, they fired several shots at us. Our cousin Paul grabbed a trash can lid in an attempt to shield us from the flying bullets. We laugh about this now, but thinking back, we are sincerely thankful no one was injured.

Before each crusade, we would advertise by tying a loudspeaker to the top of a car or pickup truck. Driving up and down the streets in the village, we would play loud music to draw the people out of their homes. Through an interpreter, we would invite everyone to come to the tent meetings. The children would fill the streets, laughing, singing, and some running behind the truck.

Gregg and our cousin Paul were out advertising the crusade in Soweto one day. They came upon a large group of people rioting. The street was blocked by large rocks and burning tires with angry people protesting the Apartheid regime in 1976. Their small pickup truck was quickly surrounded. They knew they were in imminent danger as the rioters violently rocked their truck. With the increasing sounds of pounding fists, they began to pray. Out of nowhere, a large man appeared in the crowd, approached the front of the truck, and looked at them intently. He apparently noticed the *Jesus Cares* buttons on their shirts, stretched out his arms, and shouted something to the crowd. Suddenly, the road was cleared, and they drove out safely. God spared their lives that day.

Once, we held a crusade during the winter outside of Randfontein, in Mohlakeng. This area was known for dangerous gang activity. I remember while we did our usual advertising, Jabu, who was part of our ministry team, went along with us. He was a soft-spoken young man who had given his heart to the Lord in an earlier crusade. His parents were overjoyed and asked Dad to take their son on the mission field. Their hope was to keep him away from bad influences.

One night, there was a commotion outside the tent. Some of our men came running to us, saying that Jabu had been stabbed in the chest. We immediately left the service to check on him. We learned that he had gone to a nearby convenience store to get something to eat. Jabu stood there, surprisingly calm. He told us that some guys looking for trouble started to push him around. One pulled out a knife and stabbed him. He opened his shirt, and I saw the wound. It was about an inch long, with only a small amount of blood trickling out. He suddenly became weak and wanted to lay down. We immediately rushed him to a nearby hospital, trusting the emergency room to take care of him. The next morning, we returned to the hospital to check on Jabu. We were deeply shocked when they told us he had passed away during the night.

After a few days, we checked with the police and asked if they had found Jabu's attacker. We were disappointed because, to us, it seemed they were not interested in solving the case. Was this just another gang-related incident to them? To us, it was more personal. He was one of us.

We just couldn't let it go, so we went to investigate ourselves. We finally found the people who saw what happened. We learned that his attacker was a notorious gang leader. The witnesses did not know his name but knew where he lived. Early the following day, my brothers, myself, and several of our team members went to his house with the intent of apprehending him and taking him to the police. When we got to the house, we knocked on the door. In those little houses, you could see straight through the house from the front to the back. When the door opened, he knew that we were there to get him. He ran out the back door, jumped the fence, and took off across the field.

We realized he knew his territory, and we didn't. We jumped in our vehicle and began the chase. We were determined to find this guy, and he was not going to get away. It took all day. We would spot him, and then we would lose him. Then someone would say, "he went that way," so we would go that way. The team would split up to cover more ground. There were so many little streets and many little homes, and he could be anywhere! Then suddenly, we spotted him running across a field.

Our pickup truck wasn't a four-wheel drive, but that day it became a four-wheel drive! He ran across the field, with some of our guys chasing him on foot. I was in the back of the truck, holding on for dear life. I remember him looking back and just running, running, running. Other people from the village joined the chase. It was to their benefit to find him and get him off the streets. He had terrorized the precious people of this village for far too long.

We were gaining on him. Finally, a couple of the men tackled him, and he fell to the ground. Just about that time, the police arrived and arrested him. Everyone was thankful that he was caught. The meetings ended, and the tent came down. Later on, we learned that he was fatally shot by the police as he attempted to escape during a court hearing. We were saddened to hear that this young man's life ended this way. We only wanted justice, not revenge. Our whole purpose was to share the love of Jesus, who died for all.

In 1973, we arrived in Nooitgedacht, a township a few miles outside the city of Cape Town. Dad went to City Hall to get the permit to set up the tent. He was told the place he had chosen was a battlefield for two opposing gangs and was recommended another, much safer location. Dad, however, chose to obey the leading of the Holy Spirit.

During an afternoon service, one of the workers came running to tell Dad there was a large group of men gathering close to the entrance of the tent to fight. Dad left the platform as the praise and worship continued. He walked straight toward the group of men. As Dad drew closer to the commotion, he realized that these were the opposing gangs he had been warned about. He spoke to them and was able to calm them down.

One group left, but those who remained followed Dad into the tent. Dad preached about the love of God and the sacrifice of Jesus on the cross. He shared how God demonstrated His love so all men could be free. Visibly touched by the power of God, these hardened men came forward, knelt at the altar, and surrendered their lives to the Lord. The Holy Spirit moved so deeply in their hearts that they began to lay their drugs, knives, and machetes on the altar.

This was confirmation that Dad had correctly heard from God concerning the Nooitgedacht location for the tent meeting.

11

JUST LET ME DIE

In 1982, we held a revival crusade in Vereeniging, a city about two hours south of Johannesburg. At the end of the crusade, Dad wanted to feed the people of the township. It was raining that day, so the food preparation had to be done in a large trailer. Big pots of food were cooking on portable gas stoves inside the big trailer (used to carry the tent and equipment). George went to see if he could help the ladies who were having trouble with one of the gas stoves. It was not burning properly, so he lifted the large propane tank and tilted it to see if the gas flow would improve. Suddenly, the pipe snapped and caused a massive explosion.

Gregg heard the explosion, saw the flames, and ran to help. The force of the blast threw him several yards away onto the gravel. George and the ladies were able to crawl out of the trailer to safety. They all had extensive burns on their hands and faces. George collapsed to the ground. They were all immediately rushed to the local hospital. However, because of the severity of his burns, George was transported to the General Hospital in Johannesburg. His mouth, tongue, and teeth were blackened by the fire. The shirt he wore melted into his flesh. "This man should be dead," declared one of the doctors.

His wife, Cecilia, was overcome with emotion and would not leave his side. I can only imagine how she must have felt seeing her husband in this horrific condition. I remember seeing her standing by his side, quietly praying, whispering, "Everything will be alright," as she wiped the tears from her eyes.

George said there were days when the pain was so unbearable. Every day he dreaded the nurses coming in to scrape the dead skin from his body. He could not understand why this happened to him. "This is not fair. Here I am working for you, Lord, ministering to the people, and this happens to me! Just let me die!" he cried out.

One morning as he was sitting staring out the window, feeling despondent, he heard the door open. He thought it was the nurse coming to scrape his skin again. He felt a breeze and looked to see who was there, but there was no one. He felt a Presence fill the room. Immediately there was a change. His thoughts began to change from wanting to die to, 'I don't want to die. I have a wife and little children. I still want to work for the Lord.' He then started thanking God for his healing. Later that evening, Dad, Mom, and another minister came to pray for him.

Seventeen days later, George was released from the hospital, totally healed! To the amazement of the medical team that cared for him, he walked out with no skin grafting or any other complications. He had been healed by the miraculous power of our awesome God.

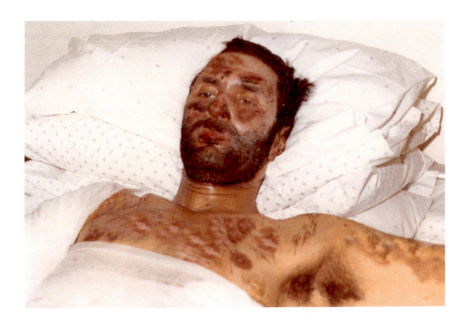

My oldest brother, George, in the hospital,
after he suffered severe burns - on his way to recovery.

October 2, 1985 - Jericho just completed a new album
Johannesburg, South Africa.

Roy, Gregg, Johan
Gershon, Manuel
known as
The One Way Band

The One Way Band
touring throughout
South Africa
- the early years

12
PICKING UP THE MANTLE

Our band, *Jericho*, returned from a recording session in Johannesburg. We were so excited about our brand-new recording project and could not wait to share it with the rest of the family. We believed this was going to be a significant step of progress for our band.

When we arrived at the butcher shop, we saw Dad's car parked in a very strange way in the road. It was an odd sight. I remember a wave of fear and terror coming over me. I knew the others must have felt the same. Something was definitely wrong. Crime was a serious problem in South Africa. There was always concern about possible acts of violence or robbery in the area.

We quickly parked, jumped from our VW Kombi, and ran into the shop. I will never forget the look on Mom's face and the sound of her broken-hearted cries. Weeping hysterically, she grabbed each one of us as she cried out, "You don't have a Dad anymore! You don't have a Dad anymore!" Shocked and confused, we could hardly believe our ears. What could she possibly mean? We don't have a Dad anymore! Is Dad dead?

No! No, this just could not be true! It took several minutes for her words to sink in. My mind refused to believe it.

I remember holding onto her as she wept and cried out. We tried to comfort her, but our precious mother was inconsolable. We were in a state of emotional shock. Having trouble comprehending what was happening, we just held Mom and cried out to God. It was the second day of October 1985 and would be one of the darkest days of my life!

Yes, it was true. Reverend George McGregor had gone to be with the Lord, almost thirty years since he answered the call of God. I remember walking into the hospital area where they had taken him. There he was, lying so still and silent – this mighty man of God. There was no breathing, no signs of life, just nothing. He was my dad! Parents aren't supposed to die so young! You somehow assume that they are going to live forever. I had just turned twenty-five years old, and I never thought of being without him. It was a devastating blow to the entire family.

Yes, I had to face a harsh reality, Dad had passed away. South Africa had lost a great son and a brave general in the army of the Lord. I remember he always said, "When the newspapers write, George McGregor is dead, don't believe them. Christians never die. They step from one life into another. It's goodbye world, and hello Jesus. To be absent from the body is to be present with the Lord."

On October 2, 1985, his heart stopped beating. He simply closed his eyes and went to be with the Lord.

Thousands of people came to the funeral service. Many came great distances and at a great personal sacrifice. We realized that the throngs of people present at the service were just a small representation of the fruits of his ministry. Looking back on Dad's life and ministry, I realized he was a tireless servant. It was not uncommon for him to preach three services a day for weeks at a time. Rev. George Edward McGregor made a difference in the country of South Africa because he was obedient to the call of God. He was like a lion coming into an area, bold and unafraid, ministering the Gospel with authority.

Even though wearing black suits to funerals was customary in South Africa, Mom requested that we all wear white. She wanted the funeral to be a celebration of his life. As Dad's coffin was being lowered into the grave, all of his children, along with their spouses and Mom, held hands and circled around the casket. Warm tears flowed down all of our faces, and our grief seemed almost unbearable as we made a vow before God. We said, "Dad, where you left off preaching the gospel of Jesus Christ, we vow this day that we will pick up the mantle and continue to preach the gospel." When the service ended, each of the brothers took shovels of dirt and solemnly completed the burial of our beloved father.

In the days and weeks following, there were serious questions about the future of the ministry. Many people wondered if the sons of George McGregor would continue in ministry or would they go their separate ways, knowing Dad was the glue that held the ministry together.

The ministry, however, did continue. We all jumped in and did the things Dad had trained us to do. Some of the brothers assumed the responsibilities of the churches that Dad had established. The tent crusades continued, although we were all thrown into deep waters. Dad was a very strong leader, and we always depended on him for guidance and direction. God was faithful through it all, and the family put their shoulders to the wheel with new zeal. By the grace of God, we kept the ministry going.

During Dad's later years of ministry, many churches were birthed in areas where he held crusades. After his passing, God placed a special anointing on Owen to carry the mantle of executive overseer. Pastor Owen and his wife Maggie worked diligently to disciple and grow these small churches. Today the satellite churches in South Africa have grown exponentially.

Rev. George Edward
McGregor born
March 12, 1926
He went to be with the
Lord October 2, 1985.

Below, his children
are dressed in white as
Mom requested. It was a
Celebration of Life
for Dad.

From left to right -
Gershon, Elize & Andrew, Johan & Raymond,
Juliet & Manuel, Joeline, Mama -
pictured at the Alamo in Texas.

13
MISSIONARIES TO AMERICA

Although we had traveled into many foreign countries on missionary ventures with Dad, America seemed to be the country God placed on our hearts. Dad seemed to have a special love for America and had made several trips there. The call to become missionaries to America began to burn in the hearts of some of the family members. It was strange that we would consider leaving South Africa to become missionaries in the greatest country in the world. After all, America sends people to the moon and has the very best preachers, singers, and musicians. For us to go there seemed foolish. America is the country that sends missionaries all over the world, not the other way around.

The burning and leading of the Holy Spirit to become missionaries to America grew stronger and stronger. The more we prayed and sought the will of God, the stronger the desire became. The whole family started praying earnestly about this calling. Manuel, his wife Joeline, Gershon, our mother, my wife Elize, and I felt sure that God was calling us to America.

We frequently got together at Mom's house as we began making our plans. We started giving away most of our belongings and equipment. We gave our musical instruments to the church and sold our cars to purchase airline tickets. To raise more money, I sold boerewors rolls (sausage rolls). One of our precious family friends, Linda Williams, worked with me throughout downtown Johannesburg selling these sausage rolls. Eventually, we raised enough money, and finally, we were going to America!

I remember how we all gathered and held hands as we prayed at the Johannesburg Airport in November 1986. We were sending Manuel and Joeline, along with their small daughter, Juliet, off to this new country. The rest of us had our tickets and promised to follow them shortly. The plans were to go to Austin, Texas, and minister with the pastor Dad met during a visit to the United States in 1983. Joeline's dad and brother lived in Austin, Texas, for a brief time. Manuel and Joeline decided to stay with them temporarily.

A few months later, my wife Elize, our sons Andrew (4) and Raymond (1), my brother Gershon, Mom, and I left to join them in Texas. I think the full impact of what we had done hit us when we arrived at the airport in New York City. We saw our children sitting on our luggage and realized that that was all we had to our names. We had left our homeland and our families and had given away just about everything we owned to follow the call of God.

We arrived in the U.S.A. on the eighth of February 1987, Elize's twenty-fourth birthday. I was twenty-seven years old at the time. We were welcomed in Austin, Texas, several hours later by Manuel, Joeline, and little Juliet. We were very excited to be in America, even though we were tired and worn out after the long flight from South Africa. We met the pastor and told him we were there to serve, to be a blessing, and to do whatever it took to reach the lost for Christ.

For the next few days, we slept in a small pull-along trailer. We needed a bigger place to stay. There was a small apartment on the church property that had been empty for several years. It was neglected and run down. Manuel spoke to the pastor and asked if there was any way we could use the place. He assured him that we would clean and fix it up ourselves. The pastor agreed and said we could live there, but we would have to pay him $375.00 a month for rent. We asked him if he could possibly make the rent a little lower for the first month or two. "If you want something cheaper," he said, "go to the projects and find something there. I want $375.00 a month." That was a lot of money for us, and our visas stated we were not allowed to work. We decided to take it by faith and moved in.

It was a very small two-bedroom apartment. Mom slept on a mattress on the floor in one bedroom, and Elize, myself, and the boys slept on the floor in the second bedroom. We didn't have a bed, mattress, table, chairs, chest, or any other furniture yet. I really think Gershon had it made though, he slept on the floor, halfway in the kitchen, and halfway in the living room.

We were more than happy to do anything the church asked us to do. Like any good evangelist, we started in the bathrooms. We cleaned, scrubbed, cut grass, and just stayed busy doing odd jobs.

Following Dad's example of going to the people, we decided to go out and evangelize in the community. We ministered on the streets, visited the hospitals, and prayed for hurting people.

For the first few weeks, we were excited to be in this new country. Things were very different in America. The language was different, especially in the South. They spoke Southern, which is a little different from the English we had learned! 'Ya'll come back now, ya hear?' It sounded so beautiful, but we didn't always understand it. The food was a little different too, black-eyed peas, cornbread, chicken and dumplings, and turnip greens. We still have to pray about the turnip green thing. Not only that, everyone drove on the wrong side of the road, and the steering wheel was on the other side of the car. It was exciting, yet all so very new to us.

The new quickly wore off and reality soon set in. We didn't have any money. Mom was with us, and Joeline was pregnant, getting very close to delivery. How were we going to support ourselves?

As young men growing up in the ministry, we had learned how to work hard and stay busy. We were still unable to work regular jobs as we had not obtained Green Cards yet. A gentleman in the church, aware of our need, asked us to help him at some of his job sites. This put food on the table and helped us to pay rent. We emptied trash cans, mowed lawns, painted, did repairs, and cleaned out apartments in the projects. While cleaning up trash and taking care of lawns, we found many needles and syringes. One day we spoke to a guy working with us and said, "From the looks of all the needles and syringes lying around this place, there must be a lot of doctors and nurses living here." He laughed heartily and said, "Man, you need to know what's going on around here." One thing was very apparent; the Gospel needed to be preached in these areas. We were beginning to understand why God had sent us to America.

We often ministered, leading praise and worship during their Sunday evening and midweek services. The pastor took up an offering for us several weeks after we arrived; however, he did not tell us the amount that came in. Instead, he told us that he would apply it to our rent. We still paid the full rent that month! We began to notice a shift in his attitude towards us and didn't understand why. We knew that changes were coming.

As Joeline's pregnancy progressed, our situation seemed to get worse. Most of the money that we brought with us was almost gone. We were very concerned. How were we going to help Manuel and Joeline? To go to a hospital would be far too expensive. A home delivery with a midwife was necessary when her son was born.

The delivery took place in the home of Joeline's dad. Elize took care of little Juliet, praying and ready to help in any way possible. Manuel and Mom never left her side, comforting and encouraging her. She had a very long, difficult delivery. We were all praying for her and the baby, as both were in danger of death. As the situation worsened, Joeline cried out, asking the Lord to please help her deliver the baby. Forty minutes later, Garner was born, weighing ten pounds and four ounces! Praise God!

14
Tough decisions

It was during this time Manuel and I urged Gershon to take Mom back home to South Africa. We could not bear to see her sleeping on the floor of our small apartment, knowing she had a beautiful home in South Africa. We were not able to provide for her and very much desired to do so. Throughout these trying times of our ministry, never once did we hear our mother complain. She was always the one who would encourage us to hold on and not give up. Since she spent most of her life on the mission field, living through some very tough times, she learned to trust God in all things.

Our return airline tickets would soon expire, and our situation was not improving. We agreed that Gershon should take Mom home. At this time, we felt it was too difficult for her in Texas. Besides, all of the family in South Africa missed her greatly and longed to see her.

We made all of the arrangements for Mom and Gershon, and soon the time came for them to leave. Feeling stuck in our current situation, Elize and I desperately wanted to get on that plane too. It seemed as if our dreams were shattered. We came with such great hope to this country and knew God called us to be missionaries, to be evangelists, to make a difference. We wanted to obey and answer the call of God. We really thought that everyone in this country would embrace us, and it was going to be wonderful, but it wasn't so. We became increasingly discouraged. Our faith was tested.

I remember Elize sharing how she felt when we first began this journey: "When Johan and I first discussed the possibility of moving to America, I realized it would mean moving away from all that was familiar to me. Even worse, it meant I would be leaving my father, brother, and sisters behind. I lost my mother when I was only fourteen, and moving to another country brought those tender memories back. It made me feel like I would be losing the rest of my family, all on the same day. The decision to move to America was probably the hardest decision that I ever had to make. I still recall the sad faces and the crying of my family at the airport as we were getting ready to depart. This was it! Our minds were made up. We were going as missionaries to the United States. Although we were firm in our decision, I still retained some sense of security, knowing that if things did not go well, we could still go back home to South Africa. We had round trip tickets that were good for three months."

"The first few months in Texas were extremely hard. The most difficult times for me to be away from my family were the important dates, such as family birthdays and special events. Many nights I could not sleep because I missed them so much, especially my dad."

"It was three months later when we took my mother-in-law and Gershon to the airport. This was a particularly difficult day in my life. As I stood there in the airport with my husband and children, my emotions were conflicted. Our return tickets would expire that very day. All we had to do was get on that plane, and in just a few hours, we would be back home in South Africa. I was fully aware that we had very little money coming in, and most definitely not enough to purchase another ticket to go home any time soon. The decision I had to make that day was probably harder than the original one to come to America. I decided to stay and tough it out to honor the commitment we had made to the Lord."

Knowing the sacrifice Elize made, walking totally by faith, and trusting God caused me to love and appreciate her even more.

As I said goodbye to Mom, I was reminded of the many times her faith was also challenged and how the faithfulness of God was proven to her over and over again. In the early days, she often questioned the wisdom of Dad's decision to give up profitable businesses to go full-time into the ministry. He always ministered in the poorest and most primitive areas of South Africa, so we had very little money and had to live by faith.

One Christmas Eve, the tree was up, the house was decorated, but there was not one gift under the tree. Everyone was excited and expecting presents from Father Christmas, but Mom knew there would be no gifts. She was heartbroken for her children and cried most of the day.

Dad would try to soothe her and say, "Mary, don't worry. God will provide." Dad prayed and reminded God of His promises, and he thanked Him for His blessings. He did not seem to worry or waiver in his faith. He just continued to pray. However, my mother was looking at eight little children with no Christmas presents, and her faith weakened as the day wore on.

Late that Christmas Eve, there was a loud knock. There stood a man at the door who said, "I need some help to bring in all these presents." He had a station wagon that was filled with all kinds of gifts, and they were all for us!

That man did not know our circumstances. No one called him or asked him to do anything. He just felt compelled to bring Christmas gifts to us. There was an abundance of toys and sweets of all kinds. Mom's eyes were now filled with grateful tears as Dad embraced her and gently reminded her, "God is faithful. Just have faith." That was the most wonderful Christmas ever.

15

THE INVITATION

For the next six months, everything seemed to be going wrong. No ministry opportunities were opening. We truly felt like giving up. Somehow, God would remind us of 2 Corinthians 11:25-27. The Apostle Paul's missionary journeys often consisted of time spent in prison; he was beaten with sticks, shipwrecked, and snake-bitten. What we were going through was not nearly as bad as what Paul had to endure. So, we took courage and kept pressing on.

I was alone in the church one evening cleaning and getting things ready for Sunday service. Suddenly, I just became overwhelmed with emotions as thoughts and questions flooded my mind. The weight of what we were going through overtook me. I sat down at the piano and just started playing – not anything specific. I found myself talking to God about how unfair things seemed to be. We didn't have any money, and we could barely pay rent on the tiny little apartment. The sad truth was, I couldn't seem to come up with any answers or solutions to our dilemma.

Tears began to run down my face as I sat there playing the piano and meditating on our situation. I felt the presence of the Lord surround me. A sweet peace came over me as words began to flow like a river from my mouth:

"Give thanks unto the Lord, give praises to His Name

And worship the Holy Spirit; glory to Jesus Christ."

Over and over, these words effortlessly flowed, and I suddenly realized I had to stop worrying, complaining, and feeling sorry for myself. The Lord just wanted me to worship and praise Him and trust Him with all my heart. He would always take care of us.

"Trust in the Lord with all your heart, and lean not on your own understanding; In all your ways acknowledge Him, and He will direct your paths." Proverbs 3:5,6 (NKJV)

I quickly ran to our apartment and told Elize that God had given me a song. I believe the message is; God doesn't want us to complain nor allow the enemy to defeat us. Instead, He wants us to praise Him and trust Him in all things.

God is always faithful! I realized He had blessed us. He had given us a 1976 Ford van, two microphones, a guitar, a keyboard, and an amp. Although they were not new, we had the tools needed to minister.

Soon after, a preacher came through Austin, Texas, and said to us, "Brothers, I love your ministry and your enthusiasm. I love what I see! Why don't you come to North Carolina and work with me? I'm an evangelist. I travel all over the United States doing large crusades. I have a big Gospel Tent, and I need your ministry." He asked that we give him about two weeks to arrange everything.

The more he talked, the better it sounded. When he said tent meetings, we said, "Wow! We love tent meetings; that is what we were doing in South Africa with our dad."

We agreed to join him in North Carolina and be part of his team. It was a ray of hope. We could hardly wait. We wanted to get out of Texas and get busy doing what God had called us to do. Two weeks went by, and finally, the evangelist called. He told us everything had been arranged and meetings were scheduled. It sounded wonderful.

We shared with our pastor and told him of our opportunity to evangelize in North Carolina. He gave us his blessings and asked if we would minister in the upcoming Wednesday night service. He told us that he would receive a special offering to help with travel expenses.

Wednesday night came. We ministered in word and song, praying with many at the altar. We shared with the congregation we would be leaving that Saturday for North Carolina. As we said our goodbyes, we were encouraged with kind and loving words. Some cried, not understanding why we were leaving. We simply could not tell them of all our hardships, trials, and disappointments, nor how our faith had been tested.

Andrew and Juliet

Joeline, Manuel, Elize, Johan

16

Duct tape and faith

Saturday finally came. It was raining as we loaded up our few possessions. Butch, a dear brother in the church, loaned us a trailer that kind of looked like a horse trailer. We securely hitched it to our Ford van.

As we were loading up to leave Texas, I noticed Joeline carrying her six-week-old baby in his little car seat to the van. Tears were streaming down her face. She was leaving her father, brother, and the security of a home behind. She was overwhelmed and whispered a prayer, "God, where will this road lead us?"

The pastor came to see us off and gave us an envelope with the offering he had received for us on Wednesday night. We thanked him for everything, prayed together, and then left for North Carolina. A few miles down the road, we opened the envelope only to discover that it contained a check for $17.00. Surely this amount was incorrect. We were dependent on that offering to get us to North Carolina. After much discussion, we decided not to go back and talk to the pastor. Instead, we prayed, "Lord, please multiply this offering." Little did we know where this road would lead us.

Many things happened on that long, hot trip. Several miles out of town, a tire blew on the trailer. We were stranded on the side of the road with no tools. Finally, we were able to wave down help and were soon back on the road. Just keeping that old van operating in the summer heat was a big challenge. It didn't have air conditioning; the brakes were bad; it was constantly overheating and smoking. At one point, the serpentine belt broke. We had no way of getting another one, and the only solution was to make a new one. We measured the broken belt, folded duct tape over and over, and stretched it around the engine pulleys. It was not a perfect fix, but it got us down the road.

We stopped in Monroe, Louisiana, for a Sunday evening service. God provided enough offering to take us further on our journey. The trip from Louisiana to North Carolina took longer than expected. Driving through beautiful mountains, we finally reached the small town of Lincolnton, North Carolina. Worn out and totally exhausted, we arrived at the home of the preacher around 1:30 a.m. This is not really a good time to arrive anywhere!

Manuel knocked and knocked on the door of the huge two-story house, but no one answered even though the lights were on upstairs. I went to knock on the back door and saw trucks, trailers, tent equipment, and dogs running around everywhere. After about forty-five minutes, we decided to drive to town and call the preacher from a phone booth. He answered the phone, telling us he did not hear us knocking, and invited us back to his house.

We drove back to the house, and he opened the door. With all of us standing there, he said, "If any of you need the restroom, come on in and do so quickly. Then I'm going to lock the doors for the night." I will never forget what he said next as he pointed outside to an old truck and an old school bus. "Find yourselves a place to sleep." We looked around. "Where did he say to sleep?" we asked one another as we heard him shut the door and lock it.

In the moonlight, we could see a pickup truck with a canopy. Manuel and Joeline decided to sleep there. When they opened the door, several dogs jumped out. It was dirty, and the odor was unbearable. Concerned for their tiny baby's health, we spent most of the night cleaning it out.

The school bus was full of old tires, tent poles, equipment, and all kinds of junk. My wife pleaded with me, "We can't sleep here, Johan." So, we slept in our van that night. I assured her, "Tomorrow morning, the sun will be out, and everything will be different. Everything is going to work out fine. Things always look better in the morning."

The next morning met us with great hope and expectation. The preacher invited us to come inside. As we stepped into his house, he said, "Wait! Stop! Take off your shoes. I just put down new carpets. I don't want stains on it."

So, we took off our shoes, went into the kitchen, and sat down. He poured us coffee, gave us biscuits, and we talked for a while.

"I couldn't speak to you last night, but our plans have changed," he said unexpectedly. "I have canceled all the revivals. There will be no meetings or tent crusades." I could not believe my ears. I asked him, "Brother, you said that there were several revivals already scheduled. What happened? We were so hopeful, and we really wanted to get busy ministering for the Lord."

He went on to explain, "My mother-in-law just came to visit, and we have planned a vacation. We are going to New York and travel the coastline from there to Florida. We will be away for several weeks." He continued, "My wife and I have a policy that when we are away, we do not allow anyone to stay in our home. So, I would appreciate it if you would be on your way again."

It felt as if he had thrown a bucket of cold water in my face. This was unbelievable! Had we heard him correctly? Our hopes had just been dashed! How could anyone do this? I remember turning around and seeing our wives crying.

We also had another problem. As we were coming over the mountains, we noticed the brakes on the van were failing. We really could not travel further without repairing them. We felt compelled to ask if we could stay another night in his yard. He agreed, so the next morning early, we went to town, purchased the parts, and repaired the brakes. Afterwards, we said goodbye to the evangelist and his family. We left there so very discouraged, questioning, "God - Why?"

We felt like the whole world was against us. We had such a feeling of desperation. Why was there nothing opening up for us? Why was there no one who could see our needs and understand our hearts' cry? Where were the Christians? Where were our brothers and sisters in Christ? Why does this land seem so hostile to us? Where do we go from here?

I prayed, "Lord, you've got to provide; You've got to show us where to go. We don't know anyone here and feel lost." For a brief moment, I wondered if we should go back to Texas. No way! We are not going back there, not right now. "Lord, please lead us!"

I remember the minute we started driving; I started praying and listening for a voice of direction. Every little town we came to, I would think, "Should we stop here? Are there Christians in this town?" Then we would go to the next town. As we approached the city of Charlotte, North Carolina, a sign on the interstate caught my attention. It read Billy Graham Boulevard. I remember saying, "Look at that sign. It is named after the famous evangelist! Wow! It is a Christian town! Perhaps the people would be wonderful and welcome us to their city and churches." We called several churches in the area; however, no one would have us minister there. We continued to drive. Hours stretched into days; days became weeks. America became a wilderness to us.

We drove from town to town and searched for a phone booth. We called churches, pastors, or any place that seemed to be a religious organization that we could find in the yellow pages. We made countless calls, using our precious dimes and quarters, calling and calling. We told them we were missionaries from South Africa and would love to come to their church to sing and minister. Some replied they needed to talk to their pastor; others said their programs were set for the rest of the year; many told us to call back next week. Sometimes they just hung up the phone. It was a daily ritual with no results. After many failed attempts, we would drive to the next town.

On one occasion, I went into a 7-Eleven store to pay for gasoline. I was whistling a tune and feeling good as I walked up to the cashier. She looked at me as she was taking a deep draw from her cigarette, then asked, "Is that your van out there?" "Yes, Ma'am," I cheerfully replied. With a smirk on her face, she said, "You've got it wrong." I looked out the window at the van, wondering if perhaps we had misspelled a word. (We had our name, *The Jerichos*, the *words Jesus is #1*, and *Missionaries from Africa to America* on the sides of the van.) She said, "It says Missionaries from Africa to America. It should say Missionaries from America to Africa." I said, "No, Ma'am, we are missionaries from South Africa." Taking a big puff from her cigarette, blowing it in my face, she asked, "What can you Africans teach us Americans?" Well, she really busted my bubble! I answered her as honestly as I could, "I know we cannot teach you much, but I can tell you that Jesus loves you. He is coming soon, and you better be ready when He does."

"Why don't you just go back to Africa?" This seemed to be a common thought among some of the churches we called. We were often told, "They need you in Africa more than we need you here."

There we were, four adults and four children traveling in this old van, without air conditioning. It was the middle of a very hot summer. We were not accustomed to the high humidity.

Where we lived in South Africa, the humidity was usually very low. The kids were crying, and we were living on practically nothing. Rest stops became our refuge. The kids could get out of the van and run and play. We could get some relief from the heat in the air-conditioned information centers.

A small ray of hope came when we were told about a Christian concert with Squire Parsons and Ernie Haase. They were also going to be serving food at the event. It was wonderful to serve our children a plate of nutritious food that night. It was here where we found a brochure that said, Music City – USA. Nashville had come up in our conversations previously. Now our wives kept saying, "Why don't we just go to Nashville, Tennessee? Nashville seems to be all about music, and we love music. We believe God is sending us there." We had also talked about going to Ohio, where our cousin and her family lived, but now, we felt certain God was leading us to Tennessee.

We were in Morganton, North Carolina, and had a long road ahead of us over the mountains. All I knew was that our van had an engine and tires, but the rest was truly held together with duct tape and faith! We prayed and trusted the Lord to bless this journey and keep our van running.

Finally, we arrived in Nashville, exited off I-40 onto Murfreesboro Road, and started looking for inexpensive motels. As one of our wives slowly drove down the street, I would run on one side, and Manuel would run on the other side, looking for the best deal. One charged $35.00 a night, another $25.00 – too much. We continued until we found one for $17.00. Maybe you've heard about motels like that. There were hairs on the sheets, roaches to deal with and bathtubs with black rings around them, broken floor tiles, and smelly sinks! What choice did we have? We checked in to the not-so-nice motel and scrubbed the bathtubs, shower walls, sinks, and anything else that didn't look clean. I would tease Elize about how picky, picky, picky she was.

The next morning, we would check out, get back into the van, find a phone booth, go through the yellow pages and start calling again. Call after call to churches produced no results. Here we were, with limited resources in a foreign country, with our wives and babies. What were we going to do? Then we asked ourselves, "What would Dad have done in this situation?" Dad had an unusual holy boldness and a quick wit. We recalled an incident that happened in South Africa that was a prime example of his wisdom and quick thinking. Dad would often hold open-air meetings in South Africa. On this particular day, the weather was beautiful, and he was preaching in a public park. A large crowd had gathered to hear the man of God preach and pray for the sick.

The people were still listening intently to the message when suddenly a traffic officer showed up on his motorcycle. He got off his motorcycle and started pushing his way to the front. Dad was standing on the steps at a monument and noticed the officer coming toward him. The officer stopped some distance away and motioned with his hand for Dad to come down from the steps. Dad looked straight at him and signaled the officer to come to him instead.

The policeman came and sternly asked, "Do you have a permit to preach out here? If not, you must stop this gathering at once!" Dad held up his bible and said, "Here is my permission." he said. "No, not that! You need permission from the City." the officer responded. Still holding the microphone, Dad asked, "Sir, are you a Christian?" "Yes!" he replied. "What church do you belong to?" Dad inquired. The policeman responded very quickly, "I'm from the Dutch Reformed Church." Suddenly, without warning, Dad threw his arms around the young officer, hugged him, kissed him on the cheek, and said, "Thank God for the Dutch Reformed Church! We are on the same side! Now, why don't you go and get permission while I continue to preach?" The policeman was stunned, jumped on his motorcycle, and sped away. Dad went right back to preaching.

We laughed as we talked about other instances we had witnessed during Dad's ministry. He told us many times that you do not have to be in a church or on a platform to preach the Gospel. Just look around you. There are opportunities everywhere. There are always people in need and ready to hear the Gospel of Jesus Christ.

The answer was obvious. He would look for a place where there were lots of people, and that is where he would minister. We knew just what to do. Where were the people in America? They were not outside in the streets, like in South Africa. They were at the malls, Wal-Mart, K-Mart, and grocery stores. The parking lots were always full of cars. So, we decided to preach to them right there.

We met with the store managers and told them we were missionaries from South Africa. We asked permission to minister outside in the parking lot to share the love of Jesus with the people. They often looked shocked, and some said no. Others said yes and allowed us to use their electricity. We set up right outside the entrance and exit door, knowing the people would have to come out at some point!

I played guitar, and Manuel used his keyboard with a small amplifier that someone had loaned us. We had two microphones but no stands! To play our instruments and sing at the same time, we needed to improvise. We used wire coat hangers, spreading the big part around our necks and wrapping the hook around the microphone to hold it in place. Now, we could sing and play at the same time.

Most of the time, we stayed from early morning till late afternoon. People would drive by in their air-conditioned cars and wave or say, "We enjoyed your singing!" The hardest part was packing up our equipment and facing the heartbreaking reality that no one had invited us to minister at their church. At the end of the day, we would still be strangers in a foreign land.

Day after day, we continued to go through the phone books calling churches, trying to find an open door anywhere. One day, Joeline and Elize saw a listing that sparked a note of excitement. "Listen! I just saw a television station listed in the yellow pages!" Joeline exclaimed. "It says, Good News Television Station. I feel like the words "Good News" are jumping out at me." Joeline called the studio, and they invited us to be guests on their show.

We were ecstatic and immediately went to the station. Sam and Joan Embry, a husband-and-wife team, were the owners of the small studio. We told them about our ministry. We ministered that day with all our hearts. Is it not amazing how God works? How awesome God is? How faithful He is even when we are not? Even when we are apt to fail, when we make mistakes and have doubts and fears - even then, He remains faithful. As we ministered, we felt the glory of the Lord come into that studio. The mighty presence of God showered on us in a glorious way as we sang and shared our testimonies. I remember watching Joan Embry, who was doing the camera work as we were singing; she wept as the anointing began to flow and had trouble holding the camera still. We were trying hard to maintain some kind of composure but seeing how she was being touched made it very difficult.

Finally, we got through the session. Joan Embry came from behind the camera and began hugging all of us. She held onto our wives and cried, "Oh, we were so blessed by your ministry. I thank God for sending you to us today."

There was no way she could have known how much we needed their ministry that day, but God knew. We didn't think we had anything to give, but again God proved Himself faithful.

We spent a little time with them, just talking and sharing. Joan Embry said, "We sing some of those same songs in our church."

When we heard the word "church," our hearts leaped with excitement! We asked, "What church do you go to?" You have to understand – we were desperate.

Her husband said, "Give our Pastor a call. Just call the church and tell him that I told you to call." He took a card out of his pocket and wrote on the back - *Millersville Assembly of God, "Home of the Happy Pastor", Paul Baggett.* We rejoiced in our hearts and thought, "Wow! Somebody is happy in America! Thank God, somebody is happy!"

We kindly thanked them and went back to our little motel to call the church. This was a ray of hope. We were happy in a cautious kind of way, but of course, we were afraid of more rejection.

"Hello, this is Millersville Assembly of God, Home of the Happy Pastor. How may we help you?" asked the friendly southern voice. Joeline told her who we were and that Sam Embry had asked us to call. She also told her that we would love to come to their church and minister in song on Sunday, or anytime. No financial demands or anything. We just wanted to minister somewhere.

The line went silent, and we thought, Oh, no! Here we go again! They are going to brush us off as so many others have done. After what seemed like an eternity, the voice spoke again and identified herself as Ramona, the church music director. "You know, our program is kind of full, but come Sunday anyway. You are certainly very welcome at our church. Our pastor loves missionaries, and one never knows what he is going to do. So, come on! I will talk to him, and maybe he will let you sing a couple of songs. No promises - just be here.", she said.

That was good enough for us! We excitedly told her that we would be there on Sunday.

We put the phone down and rejoiced with all our hearts. We shouted, praised, and thanked God that we finally had an opportunity to minister. However, this was Thursday - we soon found that from Thursday to Sunday can be an eternity when one has no money, no place to call home, and your family is in need.

We were weary of going to grocery store parking lots, tired of Wal-Mart and K-Mart sidewalks and the other places we had been going. We felt bad that our little children had to spend their days in their strollers and infant seats on hot parking lots. They had no place to play and no home to go to when the day ended. It was heartbreaking to see the anxiety on our wives' faces and hear them crying in the night. Our wives stood with us and supported us all the way, but we knew they deserved better. We knew that even when they were encouraging us, they were deeply concerned about our circumstances.

Friday came, and our money was almost gone. We had to check out of the motel where we had been staying. We called all kinds of charity organizations to see if there was a place where we might sleep and clean up. One would refer us to another, and finally, we ended up at a Catholic homeless shelter. This was a shelter for battered women and the homeless. It was located in the project area of Nashville. They immediately told us that we were welcome. They did not ask what denomination we were, why we were in need, or anything else. They just showed us unconditional love and offered us a place to eat and sleep.

As we stood in line at this shelter, we saw many people with all kinds of serious needs and desperate circumstances. They sent all the men to one side and all the women to the other side to sleep. We looked at ourselves as we stood there - healthy, strong, and able-bodied - and realized some people needed a place to stay, far more than we did. There was no way possible that the shelter had room for all the people standing in line. So, we ate a meal, thanked them, and asked them to give our beds to others who needed them more.

We walked to a park near the shelter to let the children play. It was about 7:00 p.m. I remember running down a hill with trees all around me and just weeping. I did not know what the others were doing; I only knew that I was extremely frustrated and beyond downcast. I just cried out to God, "O God! How could this be? Look at us! Look at where we are in this good and prosperous country! Look at us almost begging for a place to sleep!" Suddenly Psalm 37:25 came back to me: *"I have been young, and now am old; yet have I not seen the righteous forsaken, nor his seed begging bread."* (KJV) We all got back in the van and decided to spend the last of our money on a motel room.

The next morning, we got up and went back to the Kroger grocery store parking lot. Our hearts were so heavy. We did not want to do this again, but what choice did we have? What else could we do? We had no money left. Satan was preaching loudly to us, and we were doing a good job listening.

We drove up to Kroger at about 11:00 a.m. We stopped the van and were about to unload our instruments. This Saturday was just different. The kids were restless and crying. Despite everything Elize and Joeline did to calm them, they continued to grow more agitated, crying even louder.

The months of disappointments, hardships, and rejection had taken their toll. Suddenly, something in our wives snapped, and they started to cry! Elize asked in tears, "Don't you hear these kids crying? Don't you see how miserable they are? Can't you see that we cannot go on like this? These kids need a home, decent food, and clean beds to sleep in."

Joeline added, "No one wants us here! There is a payphone right over there. I am going to call my dad and ask him to book us plane tickets back home. You can stay, but I'm leaving, and I am taking the kids with me!"

We were all ready to give up and quit. There was no money. Our marriages were being seriously affected, and we saw nothing but defeat. It seems like when you're at your lowest point, the enemy attacks with even more force. I do not know what came over me. At that moment, I threw the van door open and ran out to the middle of the parking lot. It was a very busy Saturday morning. There were people everywhere with shopping carts filled with groceries. I found myself with my hands in the air, screaming at the top of my voice. With tears of frustration and despair running down my face, I cried out loudly to God in Afrikaans, "Here! Help ons!", which is "Lord! Help us!" in English.

Suddenly, I realized where I was. I stood there frozen, with tears still streaming down my face. I am in the middle of a parking lot in America with people everywhere. When I stopped and looked around, I saw that people all over the parking lot had stopped and were staring at me. They were probably thinking, "Who is this guy? What is he doing?" I looked toward the van; my family could not believe what I had just done. Manuel was motioning, saying, "Get back in the van, man! Get back in the van! This isn't South Africa! They will lock you up for making such a scene! Get in the van!"

I ran back to the van and just sat there, crying out, "Oh Lord, we can't go on any further. We cannot do this anymore! This is it for us!"

After a while, a calm came over us. We felt the Lord's presence even in our desperation. Manuel said, "Why don't we just drive to that church? Maybe they will help us." We discussed it and realized that it was Saturday and that there would probably be no one at the church, but what did we have to lose? So, we decided to go to the church with the happy pastor guy and see if we could find someone who could help us.

17

THE HAPPY PASTOR

We left the city of Nashville and drove north on I-65 for thirty minutes. We took exit 98, turned right, and drove to Millersville. We thought this was the smallest town we had ever seen! It did not have a traffic light or even a caution light. We wondered where in the world we were going. Finally, we saw the church on the left. The marquee read: Millersville Assembly of God | Home of the Happy Pastor | Paul Baggett.

We turned into the parking lot, but there did not seem to be anyone around. The kids needed the restrooms, so Manuel and I checked the church doors and found them unlocked. We walked into the church and immediately enjoyed the sudden rush of cold air conditioning. We could hear a faint typing sound coming from one of the offices in the back. We motioned for our wives to bring the children inside and asked them to walk in front with the babies. We thought that maybe whoever was there might have more compassion for us if they first saw women with babies in their arms. We followed the sound of the typewriter and knocked on the office door.

A very pleasant lady opened the door, smiled at us, and asked if she could help us. We told her that we were the missionaries who had spoken with Ramona a few days earlier about the possibility of singing in church on Sunday. She introduced herself as Abby Baggett, the pastor's wife. She said her husband would be arriving soon and we could talk to him.

Joeline, holding her little baby in her arms, said, "We have just one very big problem. We have no place to sleep tonight and no money left." That was a difficult thing to tell a total stranger; it was humiliating. We were all from good families and nice homes. It was embarrassing for us to have to admit we were in such desperate need.

She smiled at us, as I believe Jesus would have, and said, "That's no problem. You are welcome to sleep in our Sunday school rooms. We used to have a daycare, so we even have mats." Joeline gratefully replied, "We'll take it! Thank you very much!"

After settling in, we took the children out to play and noticed a man sitting on a rock wall, wearing jeans and a ball cap. He was shuckin' corn, as Southerners would say. He motioned for us to come over and introduced himself as Pastor Paul Baggett. He asked about our ministry, and we shared that we were missionaries from South Africa. Pastor Baggett was intrigued by our story and invited us to sing on Sunday morning. It was now confirmed – we had a booking! The Lord had opened the door for us!

He gave us a bag of fresh corn and said, "Cook it and have a nice meal. There's a refrigerator and pantry filled with food. Make yourselves at home."

After six weeks on the road, we were so grateful to have a kitchen and a place to stay. Our wives made a wonderful meal, and we settled into our Sunday school rooms for the night. We stacked the mats and made comfortable beds; however, we did not sleep much. We prayed and sought God most of the night for the upcoming service.

When we think back, we are so blessed by the fact that the first thing the man of God gave us was food and a place to stay. Again, we were reminded of the scripture in Psalm 37:25 that tells us, "The righteous will not be forsaken, and their seed will not beg for bread." (NKJV) God is faithful!

Sunday morning, we were up at the crack of dawn. We were so excited and had prayed that this would be our breakthrough. Then the devil started preaching to me. "You're just wasting your time. They are not going to enjoy your music or your ministry. Your accent is against you. You have been rejected all these months. What makes you think this time is going to be any different? Where are you going to stay tonight? Or tomorrow? You are out of money, and what are you going to do for food?" Isn't it just like the devil, when you are at your lowest, he strikes even harder? When you are in the valley, he comes with all his lies and fears.

We walked into the church and saw about 400 people packed in the sanctuary. The praise and worship started with great enthusiasm. Pastor Baggett's daughter, Alisa, led the worship and started singing, "Oh, Victory in Jesus, my Savior forever…." It was the first time I had heard this song, and I was thinking, victory in Jesus? – for you, maybe, but not for me." I still felt defeated and somewhat anxious. We had struggled for so long, and now it seemed that just maybe things could change. I usually worship God with everything in me, but not this morning.

I did not feel like singing. I did not feel like clapping my hands. I did not want to do anything. I felt like I was at the end of my rope. The pressure of the struggles and disappointments we had faced since we arrived in this country had finally come to a head – and here we were. Perhaps this is our last chance; what if we fail?

Suddenly, after one of the worship songs, the pastor stood up and, without warning or prompting, said, "We've got some friends from South Africa with us, and they are coming to sing for us. The Jerichos! Come minister to us." For a split second, we didn't move! Then we realized, "Hey, that's us! Let's go!"

Elize took charge of the kids – Andrew, Raymond, Juliet, and Baby Garner. Manuel, Joeline, and I ran to the platform. Joeline went to the piano, and I grabbed my guitar.

Joeline started playing the piano, singing; There is Power in the Blood. Not the fast tempo arrangement that we usually sing, but a slow – slow -

> *There is p-o-w-e-r, p-o-w-e-r*
> *Wonderworking power*
> *In the precious blood of the Lamb*

Immediately something changed in the atmosphere; the anointing fell! The people started jumping up out of their seats, raising their hands and praising the Lord, weeping and worshiping. Then we sang the song in Afrikaans -

> *Daar is k-r-a-g, k-r-a-g,*
> *Wonderbare krag*
> *In die dierbare bloed van die Lam*

It was as if a wave of glory hit the place. Joeline was trying to sing through her tears. I tried to sing a song by Dallas Holm, Your Heart, Your Home. But it felt like I had a tennis ball in my throat. I was weeping. Manuel, totally overwhelmed by the presence of the Lord, could hardly get understandable words out of his mouth. Because we were not able to sing our best, I thought this was our one chance, and we were blowing it!

Then Manuel took the microphone and started singing, We are standing on Holy Ground, and another wave of glory swept through the sanctuary. We were all caught up in the sweet presence of the Holy Ghost. I looked at the pastor, and he was dancing and praising God. People ran around the sanctuary; others ran to the altar and fell on their faces before the Lord! It was wild, wonderful, and awesome!

Pastor Baggett ran forward to the podium, took the microphone, and cried out in a loud voice, "God is in the house! Revival is starting now! Altar workers, come! This is revival!" Then he turned to us and said, "Now, you go lay hands on the people and pray for them."

It was wonderful! It was glorious! The people were shouting and praising God. People were being saved. Others were rededicating their lives to the Lord. It was like heaven on earth!

At the conclusion of the service, Pastor Baggett announced, "This is revival!" He turned to us and asked, "Can you be back tonight?" I knew one thing for sure – it was not time to say, "Let me check our schedule." This was our breakthrough! We said, "Yes, Pastor, we will be back tonight."

Night after night, the revival continued. Every night the pastor would tell us to be back the next night and then the next night and so on. After the second week of revival, we called Gershon in South Africa and said, "Start making arrangements to come back and bring Mama with you. We are in revival and need you!"

We continued in revival for six weeks at Millersville Assembly of God. Approaching the seventh week, Pastor Baggett decided to put up a tent across from Rivergate Mall, north of Nashville. We were in revival there another two weeks. We literally witnessed first-hand the mighty power of God. People were saved, healed, and filled with the Holy Spirit. This so reminded us of our meetings back in South Africa under Dad's big tent. We knew this was where we belonged.

We lived in the Sunday school rooms of the small church for three months. I can remember on many occasions people would knock on the door and ask, is this where the Jerichos live? Feeling led by the Lord, they would bring us bags and boxes of food. We received so much that we shared with the neighbors around us - especially the turnip greens. After all, Southerners seemed to really love their turnip greens. Thank the Lord; our needs were abundantly met day after day.

The people of the church embraced us like family and would bring us mattresses, bedding, food, plates, cups, saucers, forks, knives, and money. Elize and Joeline would sit on the floor and divide the things that were given to us. A plate for you, a plate for me; a cup for you, a cup for me. Chipped plate – it did not matter. The cup does not match the saucer – so what. Our needs were being met, and it was wonderful! We even bought a small kiddie pool to use as a bathtub. The church became our home. We stayed there for three months before we were able to find homes for ourselves.

Mom and Gerhson returned to join us in full time ministry. Mom moved in with Elize and me, while Gershon stayed with Joeline and Manuel temporarily.

We began getting invitations to go to churches to minister. We frequently traveled with Pastor Baggett on revivals, tent crusades, and brush arbors. We visited schools, hospitals, nursing homes, prisons, or anywhere that doors would open. God was blessing our ministry.

Pastor and Sister Baggett were wonderful friends and a tremendous blessing to us. They were very instrumental in helping us to establish our ministry in the United States. They brought us into their home and into their hearts. The Baggett family became very dear to all of us. Their daughter,

Alisa, and three sons - Alan, Clay, and Matthew, are all in ministry and love the work of the Lord.

We learned so much from Pastor Baggett's uncompromised preaching of the Word of God. We can truthfully say that in all the years we knew him, he never changed; Yes, he was our very own HAPPY PASTOR!

His life touched so many people worldwide, from Politicians, CEO's of major companies, and even those in the entertainment industry - such as the legendary Johnny Cash, Chad Atkins, Robert Duvall, and more. Pastor Baggett's life and ministry was the inspiration for the movie *The Apostle* written and directed by Robert Duvall - starring Robert Duvall and Farah Fawcett.

We sang a song for many years called Don't Give Up on the Brink of a Miracle. That song now holds special meaning to us. We almost gave up that Saturday in the Kroger parking lot; we were going back to South Africa in total defeat - but that Sunday morning was the beginning of our greatest breakthrough. When God has called you, never give up! When you have any need, don't give up! Press on until you get your breakthrough. Your miracle is on the way.

18

MIRACLE IN THE MEAT SHOP

We received many invitations to minister once Pastor Baggett shared the news of the mighty move of God with his pastor friends.

Along with Pastor Baggett, we were scheduled for a revival at the Living Word Church in Scottsville, Kentucky, with Pastors Marvy and Francis Wood. Still hungry for more of God, Pastor Baggett's church members filled two church vans, and several cars also followed to attend another week of powerful meetings.

Next, we traveled south to minister at Friendship Assembly of God in Victoria, Mississippi, with Pastor Sheriff. We experienced an old-fashioned brush arbor revival meeting for the first time.

I fondly remember our time in Hatchies Bottom, Mississippi, at the home of Pastor Junior and Kathy Davis. They insisted we take their bedroom while they slept on the floor in the laundry room. Their church had an old plank floor with cracks so wide you could see chickens pecking the dirt underneath. It was raining one night during service, and as we worshiped, rain would drip from the roof of that old country church onto Manuel's keyboard and the pulpit. Nevertheless, God moved mightily in that humble environment!

Gershon and Mom had to return to South Africa for a brief time while we continued revival services around the United States.

One night, after ministering in revival in the mountains of Tennessee, Elize woke me up with fear and concern in her voice. She had a dream in which she saw Gershon's and George's faces, and they were in serious trouble. It was about 12:30 a.m. when we started praying, binding the forces of evil, rebuking Satan and all his filthy works. We prayed earnestly for divine protection over Gershon and George. Later that morning, we called South Africa and learned they had been in an armed robbery around the same time we were praying.

During that time, Gershon and George were managing the butcher shop that Dad had opened in Johannesburg to help support the ministry there. Early one morning, Gershon arrived to open the butcher shop. Three men walked in. It was not uncommon for construction workers to come in to buy meat early in the morning.

Suddenly he felt the cold hard steel of a gun being pushed into his side. One of the men had crept up behind him while he was on the phone. Violently shoving and punching him, the robber demanded Gershon to go to the back of the shop. Gershon looked around for his hired help, but they were nowhere to be found. They had abandoned him when they realized an armed robbery was about to take place.

Even while being beaten, Gershon tried to make sure that he could be seen through the window, hoping someone would call the police. He caught a glimpse of George's truck and knew he would be coming into the shop soon and had no way to warn him of the danger.

One of the men held a .38 Special Revolver to Gershon's head and demanded him to hand over all the money. Another one grabbed his wallet, tore his watch from his arm, and took everything from his pockets. Gershon knew that he was very close to being killed. Suddenly, he felt a sharp, searing pain. Blood started gushing from a deep wound on his forehead. His head was spinning, and he was fighting to stay conscious. He had been struck with a gun.

Gershon recognized George's voice as he screamed in terror, "Brothers, don't shoot, don't shoot! I'm a man of God, and I have a wife and four small children. Please don't shoot me!"

As they grabbed George and drug him to the back, he saw Gershon covered in blood. He thought Gershon had either been shot or stabbed and knew he would be next. It was common to hear of shop owners being murdered during robberies. The robbers tied their hands behind their backs and started kicking and hitting them repeatedly. They threw them into the walk-in freezer and locked the door. In that cold dark freezer, my brothers pleaded the blood of Jesus and asked God to save their lives.

While they were praying, the door of the freezer suddenly opened. Two of the men came toward them shouting, "Let's finish them off now." Pointing their guns at their heads, they pulled the triggers.

They repeatedly tried to shoot, but their guns would not fire! One of the men turned and walked out of the freezer, cursing and shaking his gun. Again, he examined the gun, cursed it, and banged it against his hand. His anger grew as he could not figure out why his gun would not work. Walking back into the freezer, pointing his gun, he tried to shoot again. The gun absolutely refused to fire! Something supernatural happened – God intervened!

By this time, George and Gershon were praying out loud in the Holy Spirit and thanking God for His mercy. The robbers and would-be murderers became very confused and frightened. Finally, they ran out of the cooler, screaming, "Let's get out of this place!" By the time the police arrived, the robbers were gone.

That morning, in the freezer of a butcher shop in Johannesburg, South Africa, Jesus showed up. He stopped the guns from firing. He spared my brothers' lives, and for this, we give Him all the praise and glory. Had it not been for our Lord, they would not be here today.

A life-changing decision was made that day to sell the business and wholeheartedly trust the Lord to provide.

19

THE OFFER

Gershon and Mom had arrived from South Africa. We were all very excited to be reunited. It was always Mom's desire to be with us on the mission field, carrying on the ministry of the Gospel of Jesus Christ.

We were invited to sing at a Jerry Lewis Telethon for Muscular Dystrophy in Russellville, Kentucky, in 1988. It was a festival atmosphere, with a variety of music, food, and activities. After singing several gospel songs, we were called to the office of the Event Coordinator, who was also a Music Producer. He was dressed in true Texas fashion; oversized cowboy hat, boots, western suit, and a big belt buckle. He had a powerful presence; I could tell that he was a person of money and influence.

We sat down in his office and had a brief conversation with him. He told us, "I like what I see!" and offered us a recording contract on the spot. "You guys are going places," he continued, "and money won't be an issue." He assured us of nationwide bookings and offered us a brand-new tour bus if we signed right then. "Just read over it, sign it, and it's a done deal," he said as he slid a contract across the table. '"All you'll need to do is choose five of your gospel songs, and I'll choose five country songs for the album."

He left the room to give us time to talk it over. Bookings, a brand-new bus, money, and everything we needed were just offered to us. However, my brothers and I knew instantaneously that we could not accept this offer. We were not going to compromise our call and the vow we made to the Lord. It was all gospel or nothing, period.

When he returned to the room, he sat behind his desk and waited for our answer. We slid the contract back across the desk to him and told him we could not accept it.

"What do you mean you won't accept?" he questioned.
"We are a gospel group," I explained. "Your gospel songs and my country songs will work well together. They will sell albums. Do you know how much money we can make?" He was still trying to convince us.

We stood up and politely told him again we could not accept and then left his office.

20

THE ENEMY TOO DUMB TO QUIT

Soon after we settled in Nashville, we applied for Permanent Residency Status in the United States. It would allow us to live and work in the United States and eventually apply for citizenship. We worked with immigration attorneys with the goal of obtaining Green Cards.

For many months, it seemed we were constantly gathering, filling out, and presenting one form after another. We submitted certificates of Ministerial Training and Education, Certification of Ordination, and even more documentation. In the process, thousands of dollars were spent on attorney and immigration fees. We cooperated with the attorneys and with the U.S. Citizenship and Immigration Services in every possible way. Day after day, we anxiously watched the mail for our Green Cards.

Finally, a letter arrived from the Department of Immigration, and we excitedly opened it. The letter was from the Immigration Judge, and it read something like this:

Dear Reverend McGregor,

We are sorry to inform you that your application for residency in the United States has been denied. You are hereby ordered to leave the United States within thirty (30) days of the date of this letter. If you fail to depart the United States, deportation proceedings will be filed against you with the immigration court.

Can you imagine how we felt after all the struggles and now this devastating news? It was like the rug had been pulled out from under our feet. It felt like a bad dream.

Elize recalls, "After reading the letter, I looked at all the possessions that we accumulated since our arrival, from the furniture to the little ornaments. I realized that all this would have to stay behind, and we would have to start all over again. I was saddened by the idea of having to leave all the wonderful friends to whom we were so attached. And our children would have to leave their friends, school, and the only place they had known as home! For so long, I struggled with a sense of not belonging, but at that moment, so much changed for me. In the past, I always referred to home as South Africa. Now I realized America is home. Now we received a letter, telling us to leave. It was so hard!"

How could this be happening to us? We tried everything. Letters from churches, letters from our pastors, we wrote the Governor of Tennessee, we contacted our state representatives, and anyone else who we thought might be able to help us. Senator Al Gore assured us that he would do all in his power to help us but to no avail. The decision of the Department of Immigration was final.

Elize and I booked our flights to return to South Africa. In faith, we decided to keep our home and only take our suitcases with a few clothes. We definitely planned on returning. Despite our hopes and faith that we would be back, there was still uncertainty.

December of 1989, in less than thirty days after receiving the letter from the Department of Immigration, we found ourselves on a plane back to South Africa. There I was with my family, going back to Johannesburg. It really seemed like a major defeat. They had won, and we lost.

When we arrived back in South Africa, our families were very glad to see us. We stayed with my sister, Rosalind, and her family. Both Rosalind and Dan were such a blessing to us and tried to help in every way. I was not ready to admit defeat. I was certain that God had called us to America, and I was not going to give up that easily. Elize and I made an appointment with the Embassy of the United States in Johannesburg.

After several interviews at the Embassy, we were told that if the Immigration Courts in America already denied us, there was nothing they could do for us. We persisted, refused to accept no as an answer, and would go back to the Embassy day after day. We were repeatedly told there was nothing that could be done. We were advised to wait five years and re-apply. "Perhaps at that time, your request might be accepted," the clerk explained. We did not believe that it was God's plan for us to wait five years.

Elize and I were earnestly praying and seeking the Lord about this matter. We both felt compelled to present our case to the immigration authorities once more. We decided to set up another appointment with the Embassy of the United States.

Once again, we stood in the office of the Embassy of the United States, presenting our case with great faith and expectation. The clerk attending to us was particularly negative on this day. She reminded me that we had gone over this many times before, and nothing had changed. Raising her voice, she said, "I told you, wait five years and re-apply. Perhaps your application will be approved at that time. Please don't come back until then." She was obviously tired of dealing with us and had no intention of trying to help us in any way. As we talked with her, I noticed that a lady sitting behind the counter kept looking at me. She looked as if she wanted to say something to me and was having trouble concentrating on her work because of it.

She finally got up from her desk and came to the counter. Through the intercom, she asked, "Are you a McGregor?" I replied, "Yes, I am." Then she asked, "Is your dad a preacher?" "Yes!" I answered, feeling a bit more hopeful and excited. She continued to question me. "Is he the preacher that held big tent crusades all over the country?" By this time, I'm wondering what this lady is up to. Again, I answered, "Yes."

She broke out in a big smile and said, "I thought I recognized you as one of his sons! Your father came to our city many years ago, and I got saved under his ministry. As a matter of fact, my whole family got saved under his ministry." She then told the lady who was helping us, "I'll handle it from here. I will take care of them."

She then looked over our paperwork, told us to wait for just a minute, and disappeared into another office. Ten minutes later, we had our papers in hand, ready for an interview with the American Consulate.

Our request for permanent residency was approved! Soon we were on our way back to the United States of America. We received our Green Cards just a few days later, as we re-entered the United States in January 1990! PRAISE THE LORD FOR HIS MIRACLE POWER AT WORK!

Manuel, Joeline, and their children also had to return to South Africa and re-apply for permanent residency at the Embassy of the United States. The same precious lady who helped us also helped them obtain their Green Cards, and they too returned to the United States in a very timely manner.

We thank God for His favor and His blessings. We also thank God that the impact of Dad's prayers and ministry lived on even after he was gone from this earth. How marvelous to know that God's promises are true and His mercy is everlasting.

"For the Lord is good; His mercy is everlasting,
And His truth endures to all generations."
Psalm 100:5 NKJV

21

THE MINISTRY GROWS IN THE USA

Our ministry in America continued to grow as God began to open new doors of opportunity for revival meetings.

George, his wife Cecelia, and four children Olivia, Warren, Craig, and Grant-Ross moved to the United States and immediately joined us in Revival Meetings. Owen, Roy, and his wife Bernadette, with their two daughters, Cindy and Melissa, came to visit and also ministered with us. We were overjoyed to see more and more families arriving and were amazed to see the hand of God provide for our ever-increasing needs.

We were invited by Pastor Gary Rose to hold revival meetings in the South Fulton, Tennessee area. The power of God began to move each night with people being saved, healed, and set free from addictions. I remember two men, bound by a spirit of homosexuality, were gloriously delivered. It was the kind of revival that really stirred up the devil.

The last night of the revival had a big emphasis on praising and thanking the Lord, no matter the current circumstances or what the next day may bring. We challenged the crowd to praise God, just as Paul and Silas praised Him, even while they were chained and in prison.

We traveled home from the revival to Nashville on I-24 in two separate vans. Elize and I, with our three children, George, and his twin boys, were leading the way. Gershon, Owen, Manuel, and Joeline, with their two children, were following in the other van. After about two hours on the road, we heard Manuel's voice coming over the CB radio, exclaiming, "Pull off the road! There is smoke coming from your van!"

It was about 2:00 a.m. as we pulled off onto the shoulder; the other van pulled in behind us. I jumped out of the van and opened the hood. Just as I did, fire and thick black smoke engulfed the whole engine compartment, knocking me backward, burning the palms of my hands. All I could think about was my wife and children inside, fearing it could explode at any minute. I quickly ran to the side door of the 1986 Chevy van, threw open the door, and shouted, "Get out! Get out! The van's on fire!"

We grabbed the kids from the van and quickly got them a safe distance away onto the grassy banks of the highway.

The flames were quickly spreading. Our six-month-old baby son, Brandon, was strapped inside his car seat, and we struggled to loosen him as raging flames started to rush throughout the inside of the vehicle. There was no time to save anything else - handbags, purses, wallets, cameras, guitars, and the entire week's offering that we had just received from the church – nothing could be retrieved as flames totally engulfed the interior within seconds!

We had a big trailer hitched to the van, loaded with our suitcases, some musical instruments, and our sound equipment. What were we to do? We knew the van had a full tank of gasoline and could explode at any moment. The heat and force of the flames were uncontrollable! The windows were bursting out, sending glass and debris flying through the air.

With the fury of the flames sweeping through the entire vehicle, we made a quick decision. Being fully aware of the danger, we chose to ignore the loud crackling sounds and unbearable heat of the raging fire and proceeded to unhitch the trailer, pushing it to safety.

All we could do was watch as our van was burning to the ground. Our wives and the children were all crying in shock. The Fire Department arrived within minutes though it seemed like hours.

As the fire was raging, we did something very strange. We raised our hands and started singing and praising the Lord right there on the side of the road. I know this must have looked crazy – praising God when your van, money, and personal belongings were going up in smoke.

The firefighters stared at us in total disbelief as they put out the flames. I'm sure they thought, "How could these people be praising and thanking God at a time like this?"

The van was a total loss, so we all piled in the other van. We thanked God from the bottom of our hearts that we were still alive and well. We drove home, secure in the knowledge that God would somehow provide another van for our ministry.

We immediately realized our Green Cards were in Elize's purse and destroyed in the fire, creating a real problem for us. To replace them was both complicated and very costly. We had to have our Green Cards. Days later, as Elize and I prayed about this dilemma, she told me that we should find the van and go through the ashes. To me, this seemed like a foolish thing to do; obviously, nothing could have survived those flames. She would not give up on the idea, even when everyone told her it was a waste of time. Fire hot enough to burn up a vehicle and everything in it certainly would consume any paper or plastic items in a flash.

Elize was persistent. She strongly felt we should go find the van, expecting to retrieve our Green Cards. Finally, we went to the salvage yard and found the burned-out van. It was truly a sad sight, a skeleton of metal, filled with soot and ashes. We began to sift through the ashes looking for anything that might have been spared in the hot flames. We combed through the charred remains for a long time but found nothing.

Just as we were about to give up and go home, I felt compelled to look one more time where Elize had been sitting in the van. As I poked around, I felt something hard. Incredibly, it was the charred remains of Elize's purse. The outside of the purse was totally destroyed, but as I pried it open, there inside laid the Green Cards, along with the revival offerings. They were miraculously untouched by the fire. We both just started thanking God as tears ran down our faces, and we could not wait to tell everyone about this wonderful miracle.

"I will bless the Lord at all times:
His praise shall continually be in my mouth."
Psalm 34:1 (NKJV)

22

OUR SWEET MOTHER CALLED HOME

Mom was a devoted woman of God, passionately in love with Jesus. She wholeheartedly supported Dad and his ministry. My parents had a strong marriage, and I never heard her raise her voice to him. I always admired the way Mom showed her love and devotion to Dad. She deeply cared about how he looked as he ministered by making sure his shirts were freshly pressed and his shoes were shined. I also remember how she cared in simple ways, like setting aside the best fruit and telling us that it was for Dad.

Mom had a servant's heart. Dad often brought in the homeless who needed food and clothing. She always welcomed the needy with open arms, prepared a good meal, and would draw them a hot bath. Even with eight children to care for, she would find time to go through her or Dad's closet to give them clothing and shoes. My older siblings recall when Mom would take sheets of newspapers and fold them to place inside her own worn-out shoes with holes in the bottom and give away her good shoes. She even took the time to wash and style the women's hair, providing them with a sense of dignity. Many were then able to find employment or return to their families and communities.

The way Mom supported Dad in ministry, she also supported her children in their ministries. During the services, she covered us in prayer, asking the Holy Spirit to have His way. She was also faithful to help pray with people in the altars. When she traveled with us in the United States, we welcomed her wise counsel. She would often remind us how our father would have handled certain situations. Her wisdom was astonishing and still helps guide us today.

On May 26, 1992, after a short illness, our dear mother went to be with the Lord at only sixty-seven years old. I remember Mom's last words to us, "Always love one another." She was a wonderful, loving mother and grandmother. Her grandchildren adored her. She knew how to make a house a home. She held our trust, and we appreciated and respected her advice, judgment, and character. We deeply mourn her passing, as did her family and friends in South Africa and the United States. We still miss her greatly today. Even though Mom was buried in Nashville, Tennessee, and Dad was buried in Johannesburg, South Africa, we know that they are together forever with the Lord.

23

BREAKTHROUGH

As God began to move mightily in our meetings, doors opened, and we were invited to hold revival meetings all over the nation. Our calendar, which was empty for so long, was now booked two years in advance.

In 1993, news of our style of gospel music reached a major recording company in Nashville, Tennessee. A producer of a very reputable recording company offered us a recording contract which we accepted. It was during this time that we became known as The McGregors. Our music was lively and unique with its dynamic, uplifting South African flavor. It captured the interest of people across denominations, ages, races, and cultures.

As our music gained national attention, we were showcased at the National Quartet Convention in Louisville, Kentucky. Several of our songs reached the top of the gospel music charts. We became regular guests on well-known television shows, radio programs, and gospel concerts.

One of the most popular albums we recorded was Yes Lord. Voice Magazine nominated this album as Album of the Year and nominated The McGregors for The Sunshine Award - Group of the Year.

1999 was a breakthrough year for me personally, as my family and I became citizens of the United States of America! We had waited so long for this privilege and will be forever grateful.

Also, in 1999, The Brooklyn Tabernacle Choir recorded a song written by Manuel and Joeline called, 'We Are United'. This song is on the Brooklyn Tabernacle Choir Grammy Award-winning album High and Lifted Up. We have also been privileged to sing at the Brooklyn Tabernacle in New York with Pastor Jim Cymbala on numerous occasions, as well as many of her sister churches in the area.

Our ministry began to receive invitations for Crusades, Pastor's Retreats, Men's Fellowships, Women's Conferences, Youth Rallies, Camp Meetings, and Revivals. Many times, we were invited to share our South African history, culture, music, and testimony in the public schools.

We often ministered in prisons to hardened criminals. One such prison was the infamous Brushy Mountain Prison in Morgan County, Tennessee. I remember walking through the security clearance with my brothers Gershon, Gregg, Manuel, and Roy, following the armed guards into a large area where about one hundred inmates stood waiting to hear us. Being in a maximum-security prison was very intimidating, to say the least.

As we began singing our South African songs, they began to smile, clap their hands, and move their feet to the beat. After sharing the love of Jesus, many prayed and asked Jesus into their hearts. At the end of the service, a tall, intimidating man approached us. He was visibly moved to tears asking if God could ever forgive him for what he had done. He shot four men in a bank robbery. We told him that if he truly repented and meant it when he prayed the prayer, then God had forgiven him.

"If we confess our sins, He is faithful and just to forgive us our sins, and to cleanse us from all unrighteousness."
1 John 1:9 (NKJV)

I remember on our way back from Revival Meetings in Columbus, OH, we stopped at a gas station to fill the van. As I ran into the building to pay, the woman behind the cash register heard me whistling a tune and said, "You're awfully happy"! I replied, "Yes, ma-am, we just finished revival meetings a few miles from here, and God did so many wonderful things." As I was still talking with her, tears began to flow from her face. She told me how her life was falling apart, her husband had left her with three small children, and she's doing everything to barely make ends meet. "Please could you pray for me," she asked. I reached over the counter and began praying for her. The Holy Spirit touched this dear lady as she began weeping and shaking. Then I heard someone else shout, "Pray for me too!" It was another woman packing shelves, and I went over to pray for her too.

Another time, we were at the airport in Cleveland, Ohio. It was a Saturday morning. Gershon, Manuel, and I were running to our gate to make the flight back to Nashville, TN, when I heard a man shout, "Hey!!" When I looked to see who it was, it was a man working at the ticket counter for Delta Airlines. He left the counter with people in line and came to where I was, standing in the aisle. He said that he was in our Friday night service and desperately needed prayer. He said that he was an alcoholic and needed to be set free. His whole life was falling apart because his wife left him, and she took the children. He did not go forward for prayer and knew that he had missed God. He said he begged God the night before to help him and to give him a second chance. So when he saw us the next morning running past him, he knew that this was his opportunity for a miracle. I took him by his hands and began to pray that God would set him free and restore his life and home.

It was about a year later that we returned for revival meetings at the same church when a man came and threw his arms around me. At first, I didn't recognize him. He explained he was the man at the airport who I prayed for last year. He was completely transformed by the power of God. His wife returned home, and now his whole family is serving the Lord.

24

THE OLD FARM HOUSE

The year 1995 marked ten years since our dad's passing. The church in South Africa wanted to honor his memory with a banquet and a special memorial service in Johannesburg. As plans were put into motion, many people throughout South Africa expressed a desire to be included in this celebration of his life and ministry. All the brothers made plans to travel to South Africa for this very special occasion. We also invited friends from the United States to join us for this celebration.

Soon a tour was arranged for the McGregor Brothers to visit many of the cities that Dad had evangelized. One of the places we were to visit was our old home, located in the Paarl area. The old farmhouse where we lived for many years was still standing and scheduled to be turned into a home for the elderly by the city of Paarl.

This old house had become somewhat of a legend in the Paarl area. The local people had many stories to tell of the fond memories they had of Rev. George McGregor, his family, and their home. Dad was well-known for his many acts of kindness and generosity. It was not unusual for him to bring people to our home who needed food, a place to sleep, or financial help. Those who were sick and in desperate need of prayer would often show up at our door. No matter what time of the day or night, Dad would never turn anyone away.

The news of the old McGregor farmhouse being transformed into a home for the elderly was to be released to the public. Reporters from the local newspapers and radio stations contacted us and asked to meet there for interviews and pictures with the McGregor family. The committee in charge of the plans for the transformation was to meet us there as well. It was a wonderful thing, and we were certainly honored.

Just thinking about going back to our old home was very exciting. I had not been there in twenty years. I was just a young boy when we moved from the farm to the city of Johannesburg. Many wonderful memories flooded my mind, and I started to pray silently for a very personal, special request. I asked the Lord to let me find something of Dad and Mom, some form of tangible evidence of my childhood memories. The farmhouse had been bought and sold several times since our family had moved away, and several different families had lived there during the span of the past twenty years.

We drove into beautiful Paarl in November 1995 with our friends from the United States, relatives, as well as many old friends who joined us for this special occasion. As we drove along the winding road through the beautiful rolling hills and lush green vineyards, emotions and memories washed over me like a flood. Suddenly, we were there, and again I whispered the same prayer, "Lord, let me find something ... anything."

Reporters, photographers, and other news media were already there when we arrived. They were snapping pictures and immediately began asking questions.

The landscape had drastically changed. Many new homes had been built on what was once beautiful vineyards and fertile farmland.

The house was well-kept and in good shape. Manuel remarked that the floor tiles in the kitchen were the same as they were when we lived there. He remembered this vividly because it was often his chore to clean this floor!

Excitedly, we took our friends through the house, sharing our childhood experiences, laughing and crying as we traveled back in time with our memories. We pointed out the living room, with its original hardwood floors, where the family used to pray. I remembered Dad's prayers distinctly echoing through the house, day or night. If Dad were home, you would most likely hear him praying. I used to wonder, "When does Dad ever sleep?" We also pointed out the large room where all the brothers slept and the room my sister Rosalind had all to herself, being the only daughter.

Still hoping to find something, I quietly left the group and slipped outside. I climbed up the stairs leading into the attic. I was looking for something, anything that had belonged to us. The attic was empty, but I remembered that as children, we often played there even though it was used for storage. I looked everywhere, every crack and crevice, and found nothing. After all, it had been twenty years, and many people had come and gone in that time. Probably many children, just like us, had played up there. It would be a miracle if anything survived or remained undiscovered.

As I ran my hand along a ledge in the attic ceiling, I felt something. It felt like papers of some sort. I pulled the papers out and started looking through them to see what I had found. I could hardly believe what I was holding in my hands! It was Dad's Ministerial Ordination papers! The photograph of Dad attached to the official documents was in wonderful condition; both the print and the ink signatures on the documents were preserved and readable!

With tears of joy running down my face, I bolted down the stairs, waving those documents in my hand. The reporters were astonished as I shared my silent prayer and discovery. They started taking pictures and asking questions again. Our friends and relatives were weeping with joy as they grasped the magnitude of the moment. It was a miracle, a wonderful blessing from above. God graciously honored the desire of my heart.

25

THE GREAT PENSACOLA OUTPOURING

In 1995, Pastor John Kilpatrick invited our ministry to come to his church for two revival meetings. The first was scheduled for May and the second for June of the same year. It was very unusual for a church to book two revivals so close together. We heard wonderful things about Pastor Kilpatrick and anticipated ministering at Brownsville Assembly of God in Pensacola, Florida.

Sunday morning, May 7, 1995, was our first service. As we were waiting to be introduced to the congregation of over two thousand, the youth pastor, Richard Crisco, walked to the podium and announced the passing of Pastor Kilpatrick's mother. Even though she had been sick for a while, the news came as a shock. She had been a pillar in the church, and the people loved her dearly. There were many tears, and a somber atmosphere filled the sanctuary, which made ministering a challenge. Our hearts went out to Pastor John and Brenda, remembering our own mother's passing.

Despite the unexpected circumstance, we ministered in song, and Manuel preached a message about the giants in our lives. When the invitation was given, Cathy Wood limped to the altar for prayer. She suffered from constant pain in her knees and hips from degenerative arthritis. Manuel asked her to name the giant in her life, but before she could say, arthritis, the power of God touched her, and she fell to the floor, instantly healed. She later wrote a book, The Visitation, sharing this testimony.

After the service ended, we thought the pastor would want to reschedule the remaining days of the revival meetings. Instead, he sent word, with his son Scott, for us to continue. His mother had been a strong prayer warrior and had fervently prayed that God would send revival. We continued to minister for the next few days, even though Pastor Kilpatrick was not present. On Wednesday morning, the congregation gathered at the church for her funeral, and in the evening, we had our last service. Through this difficult time, God comforted and encouraged the hearts of the people.

A few weeks before returning for our second week in Pensacola, God had given me a vision while in Chico, California. We were gathered at a church on Saturday night, praying in preparation for the services on Sunday morning. All of a sudden, it was like a movie playing. I saw something that I had never seen before in my life. I saw fields that looked like they were burnt. They were dry and barren as far as I could see. I was concerned and thought someone ought to do something, or otherwise, they were going to lose everything. The farmers will have a failed crop. Whatever they had planted was tall, but it was brown and dead. As I looked across the fields, I saw big irrigation pipes stretching from one side of the field to the other. The nozzles barely dripped water and I knew that this small amount of water would have no impact on the crops. They were stopped up, and I felt I needed to do something. I grabbed a sharp object, and I found myself climbing this big water pipe. I was going to move my way across this high pipe to every nozzle, but there were too many of them. With a sense of urgency, I motioned for my brothers to come and help.

As I crawled on top of the pipe and came to the first nozzle, I hit it, jabbed it, pierced it, and suddenly water gushed out. At the same time, I heard a big sound like an explosion. And I thought, "Oh my goodness, that's the beginning of where this big pipe starts." I could hear and feel the rumbling of the water in the pipes as it gushed forth, flooding the whole field. At the time, I didn't fully understand the meaning. However, I was more than ready to see the outpouring of the Holy Spirit that week in Chico.

Sunday morning, we were full of faith and expecting the fire of God to fall. As we were ministering to the large crowd, we noticed the section designated for the deaf and motioned them to come forward for prayer. We were bold in our faith and believed that God would give them a miracle. Very quickly, an usher, sent by the pastor, came to us and told us not to pray for them and leave them alone. It felt like I had been punched in the stomach and all the wind knocked out of me. I was totally shocked by this. However, we continued to minister for the rest of that week.

Sunday, June 11, we returned for the second week of revival at Brownsville. It was during this time that Pastor John and Brenda Kilpatrick introduced Gershon to Jeanne Trussel, a young lady in their church who would eventually become his wife.

Pastor Kilpatrick shared that he and his church had been praying fervently for over two years for revival. He appeared to be a man longing for answers, earnestly petitioning God with all his heart, yet there was unmistakable sadness in his eyes. The stress of his mother's illness and subsequent death, and the day-to-day pressures that come with pastoring, had left him with a heaviness of heart he could not seem to shake. Having been brought up in the ministry, we understood the pastor's heart. We knew that he was crying out to God as a shepherd and needed to see a real move of God in his church and his own life. We began praying, especially for Pastor Kilpatrick and his family.

The people of the church were hungry. As we ministered that week, the congregation was attentive to the preaching of the Word and seemed to be touched by our music. However, they were very quiet and reserved during worship. We, on the other hand, were more accustomed to seeing people show more expression by clapping their hands and dancing. I had learned over the years through Dad's ministry how important it is to get the people to engage in worship. This involvement helps each person encounter the presence of God and builds their faith, making it easier to receive. We invited the people, particularly the youth, to gather around the altar during praise and worship. We encouraged them to give God liberty to move in their hearts. The youth responded, and things began to happen.

One night we asked all the teenagers to come onto the platform. They began to passionately worship, and soon the power of the Holy Spirit began to move. As the anointing flowed, they began to weep and cry out to God. Many were filled with the Spirit in a new and powerful way. Because of the supernatural way the Lord moved that night, many of the young people's hearts were renewed, revived, and refreshed. It was years later that Mike Motley shared; he was one of the teenagers greatly touched by God that night and called to the ministry. He eventually became one of the worship leaders at Brownsville Assembly of God.

These services would sometimes last late into the night. The altars would fill with children and teens who were being visibly touched by the Holy Spirit. Many were speaking in tongues, some laying on the floor, and others standing with hands lifted high praising the Lord. While their parents waited, the Holy Spirit moved on them as well.

It was wonderful! We saw some miraculous things happening. Relationships were restored, wonderful healings, many salvations, and a fantastic renewing of hearts. We witnessed a breakthrough as people opened up to receive. As we closed out the services that Wednesday night, we all knew God had done something very special. The spiritual atmosphere had changed, and revival was emerging. However, no one had any way of knowing how God was about to move and use this church to impact the world.

Evangelist Steve Hill was scheduled to preach the following Sunday, on Father's Day, June 18, 1995. He had recently had an encounter with the Holy Spirit in Brompton, England, and the people were anticipating his testimony. That Sunday morning, the dam burst and the floods of revival rushed into Brownsville Assembly of God in Pensacola, Florida! That one service turned into a five-year revival!

As I reflect on the vision I had in Chico; the meaning was vividly revealed to us during this revival and confirmed by

Pastor John Kilpatrick. He later shared in many interviews that God used the ministry of the McGregors to help water the ground for what has now proven to be the longest revival in America since the Azusa Street Revival, the Great Pensacola Outpouring.

A quote taken from:

https://brownsville.church/about-us/history

"Setting the Atmosphere for Revival

Just prior to revival, the McGregors, South African brothers ministering in powerfully anointed music ministry, visited Brownsville to conduct a series of revival services. The heightened presence of the Holy Spirit during these services led many to wonder what might be happening in the spiritual realm, and when revival shortly broke out, the consensus was that these services had done much to prepare the spiritual atmosphere for God's mighty visitation."

The McGregors at Brownsville Assembly of God,
Pensacola, FL

Awake America Crusades - with Pastors John Kilpatrick,
Steve Hill, Lindell Cooley, The McGregors

26

REVIVAL, REVIVAL, REVIVAL

As the word began to spread, people started coming to Pensacola, standing in long lines for hours, waiting for the doors to open. They came from all over the world and from all walks of life; some older women dressed in their Sunday best, men covered in tattoos, and teens in shorts and t-shirts. I remember thousands of people filled the main auditorium and the overflow rooms, hungry for a move of God.

A dear friend of ours, Lindell Cooley, led worship every night with complete freedom. He is one of the most gifted and anointed praise and worship leaders of our time. The glory of God was upon him, and people were touched deeply in every service.

Evangelist Steve Hill preached strong, heartfelt, repentant messages and many people felt convicted and rushed to the altars when the invitation was given. Each night, during the altar call, Charity James, one of the church teens, passionately sang Mercy Seat. The altar was packed as many repented, and tears streamed down their faces. Some fell out in the Spirit, and others shook uncontrollably under the power of God. Numerous people were set free from drugs, alcohol, and other addictions. Lives were changed, and many were healed!

The effect the Brownsville Revival had on McGregor Ministries was astonishing. After revival broke out, we made it a point to attend these services as frequently as our schedule would allow. Many times, we would travel through the night just to be in these powerful evening services. You could not walk into the building without being impacted by the power and the presence of God.

The desire of our hearts in ministry had always been for revival. It was the driving force of our coming to America. The way God moved at Brownsville was on a level that we had not seen in America thus far. In South Africa, we were accustomed to seeing large crowds responding to the message of Jesus, dramatic miracles, and demons being cast out. On the contrary, in this revival, Christians were being awakened, refreshed, and empowered by the Holy Spirit. I saw pastors, youth ministers, and laymen from different denominations press into the altars, hungry for a move of God in their own lives and their churches. It has been said that during times of revival, cold and complacent Christians always get revived before sinners get convicted.

I remember how strong the presence of God was on us as we left Brownsville, traveling to Frankfort, Kentucky, for revival meetings. That Sunday morning at the First Assembly of God, Pastor Brannon invited us to the stage to minister. Something shifted in the atmosphere the moment I started to strum my guitar. Before I could even get the first words out of my mouth, it felt like a cloud burst over me, and I fell facedown with my guitar in hand. I don't remember much of what happened after that. It must have been about twenty-five minutes or more of me just weeping and praising God. When I finally gained my composure, I noticed that the rest of the congregation, including the pastor and those on the stage, were either on their knees or flat on the floor worshipping God. There was a visible move of the Holy Spirit, in a way that I had not seen before in our meetings.

As we ministered in different churches around the U.S., we noticed not every church was open to the moving of the Spirit in this way. Many of our brothers and sisters in our Charismatic and Pentecostal churches have a certain idea of the way things should work. "We grew up in this, and we're not changing," they'd say. But oh, praise be to God, we saw Holy Spirit breaking all those traditions of men.

During this time, many pastors from around the nation asked John Kilpatrick and Steve Hill to bring the entire Brownsville Pensacola Revival Team to their cities - from Dallas, Texas;

Anaheim, California to Toledo, Ohio. These meetings became known as the Awake America Crusades. The large auditoriums and stadiums were packed with people hungry for a move of God. Lindell Cooley would lead the people into praise and worship, and then we would minister in song. My brother Manuel wrote the song Lord, Revive America Again, which we sang there often:

Two hundred years or more, America was born.
She was founded on the Word of God.
So many have fallen away since that historic day
But people of the red, white and blue
Nations are praying for you

Lord Revive America again,
Let her be the lighthouse of the world one more time,
But even if You have to bring her to her knees,
Then Lord, please revive her again".

Mighty men and women of God
Were born in the land of the free
Raising up a standard for God and liberty
So many others have taken this gospel through this world,
But America, you've turned your back on God.
America, you've got to turn around,
If you humble yourself in the sight of God,
Then He will heal your land."

We were honored to travel all over the nation with Pastor Kilpatrick and Evangelist Steve Hill in the Awake America Crusades. We praise God for the thousands who were touched by the mighty power of God. And the thousands who came to know Jesus as their Lord and Savior.

Soon after the Awake America Crusades, the Lord began to open doors internationally for our ministry. We were invited to minister in Amsterdam, Holland, along with Brenda Kilpatrick, John Bevere, and Andre Crouch at the Euro Spirit Conference. Many pastors came from The Netherlands, Sweden, Denmark, France, Germany, and England, all desperate for a move of the Holy Spirit in their churches and nation.

We saw the same outpouring of the Holy Spirit on the precious people of Singapore and Malaysia as we ministered the love of Jesus in these countries. They were so receptive and gracious, eagerly hanging on to every word we preached. Even though we were not allowed to share our faith with people on the streets of Malaysia, many came to the churches held in office spaces in high-rise buildings. We saw Muslims and Buddhists accept Jesus as savior and Lord during these meetings.

27

THE PAIN THAT BROUGHT FEAR

In 2001, we were traveling extensively from city to city, holding revival meetings. It was not uncommon for me to be home only one or two days a week.

I started to have persistent pain in my stomach. At first, I tried to ignore it, hoping it would go away. As it continued into the second week, Elize urged me to see a doctor. Reluctantly, I agreed and scheduled an appointment. The doctor started pressing and poking on different areas of my stomach while asking all kinds of questions. He scheduled several tests. He finally uttered the words that would turn my whole life upside down.

"Mr. McGregor, this does not look good. I'm going to do more tests and take some samples and send it to the lab, but I'm afraid it looks like colon cancer."

The moment the doctor said those words, it felt like my whole world had just changed. I was in a cold sweat as I left the doctor's office. For the next several weeks, I couldn't sleep. My mind was racing with the most fearful thoughts.

"I'm going to die, and if I die, who will raise my children? My wife will marry some other man. What will become of my ministry? What about the call of God on my life? It doesn't make sense." On and on, day after day, night after night, this panic would not relent.

I remember going to Germany with my brothers, Gershon and Manuel, to preach a revival at Ramstein US Military Base. We saw the hand of God moving and many of the military personnel and their families were touched and transformed by the power of God. However, each night after the meetings, I was unable to fall asleep as the thoughts would come haunting me again. The doctor's words held me captive, tormenting my mind as I replayed them over and over again.

I would lay there wide awake, staring into the night, longing for daybreak, crying out to God, "Please let me sleep, even for just an hour or two." The hours would slowly pass: one, two, three, four a.m., still no sleep, no rest, only thoughts of despair and death. The thoughts were worse than the pain I was experiencing.

The following week, we returned to the US for revival meetings at Bellview Assembly of God in Pensacola, Florida. My son, Andrew, was a student at the Brownsville School of Ministry. I stayed at his apartment during those meetings, while Gershon and Manuel stayed at a hotel. The tormenting thoughts persisted. One night after the service, we were driving back to the apartment, and I heard on the radio a preacher saying something about God's accelerated miracles. I asked Andrew, "Who is that preacher?" He told me that it was Dr. Christian Harfouche, a pastor of a local church in the area. I asked him to drive by the church. It was already after 9:30 p.m., and the service was still in progress.

We walked into the church and sat down in the back. Suddenly, the preacher said, "There's someone here, and you've had a bad report from the doctor. Don't believe it!" As he continued to prophesy, he spoke the very words the doctor had said to me. I leaned over to Andrew and whispered, "It's me he is talking about." I immediately got up and began to make my way down the aisle to the altar. The pastor stopped me halfway and continued to prophesy life over me. He told me not to let fear torment me but only to believe the Word. He declared that God had great plans for my life and ministry. As I made my way back to my seat, an unexplained peace swept over me. I knew in my heart that something had changed.

A few days later, after we returned to Tennessee, I went by the post office. As I was driving home, I noticed a letter from the doctor's office. My heart raced as I slowly opened it and began reading the results. Tears flowed down my face as I read, "Negative! Negative! Negative!" all the way down the list. All I could say was, "Thank You, Jesus, for this good report." I cried, then laughed, then began to sing and praise the Lord.

I learned a valuable lesson, not to believe nor internalize negative, destructive words. Our thoughts must not be allowed to run rampant. They must be harnessed, and as scripture says, "Casting down arguments and every high thing that exalts itself against the knowledge of God, bringing every thought into captivity to the obedience of Christ." 2 Corinthians 10:5 NKJV

Charles R. Swindoll said, "Life is 10% of what happens to you, and 90% of how you react to it." The enemy wanted me to believe it was all over and to give up. He wanted me to come into agreement with the doctor's words. I have since learned what a powerful thing it is to speak life into hopeless situations and come into agreement with the Word of God.

28

A NEW SEASON

After many years on the road as missionaries and evangelists, God began preparing my family and me for a new season in ministry. My heart longed to see people encouraged, discipled, and empowered. I wanted to walk with them through the seasons of life and build community.

In 2005, we began renovating part of our ministry office in White House, Tennessee, into space for a church. After pastoring there for just a few months, we quickly outgrew the facility and moved a short distance to the vacant Millersville Assembly of God church building, then owned by a local bank. By this time, our oldest sons, Andrew and Raymond, had graduated from the Brownsville Revival School of Ministry. They were now actively involved in our church and youth revival meetings. Brandon, Chantelle, and our twin boys, Justin and Jonathan, still in school, became very involved in youth ministry and school evangelism as they got older.

On May 2, 2010, a massive flood hit the entire Nashville area and the surrounding communities. Many homes and businesses were flooded, including the Opryland Hotel. Millersville was greatly affected. For several weeks, we opened our church to people in the area whose homes were flooded and provided food, shelter, clothes, and other much-needed items.

Following the flood, Millersville became somewhat of a ghost town after many people relocated, forcing businesses to close. We then moved the church back to White House and rented the community auditorium. About a year later, our dear friend, Sister Edna Jackson, called and excitedly told me that the Lord had spoken to her that morning while she was washing dishes.

"There is a church in Lebanon, Tennessee looking for a pastor. The Lord told me that you are supposed to pastor that church." Then she added, "Now Brother Johan, you know the Lord speaks to me." "Yes, Sister Edna," I replied. "I know the Lord speaks to you, but I'm already pastoring a church." She replied, "I know, I know, but this is what the Lord told me to tell you. You have to call them, ok?"

A few days had passed, and I got another call from Sister Edna. "Have you called that church yet?" "No, Ma'am," I said. "I'm still praying about it, but I will call them, I promise."

After the third reminder, I reluctantly made the call to meet with the Board of Elders of Love's Way Community Church. As we walked into the humble little chapel, Elize and I were not quite sure this was what God had called us to.

"This is a dying church with mostly old people." one of the board members expressed at the meeting. "If God does not do something, we will have to close the doors and shut it down."

The church met at Joseph's Storehouse, a faith-based food distribution ministry started by Brother Bob and Sister Peggy Evans. We toured the warehouse seeing racks of food. Off to the side were large yellow wheelbarrows that would be overflowing with food on giveaway days. What began with just a few canned goods now fed hundreds of needy families in Wilson County and the surrounding areas. The heart of this ministry felt so familiar to me because it was what I was a part of growing up. The Lord laid this same ministry on Dad's heart in South Africa, feeding the masses in many of his crusades.

The Board of Elders knew we were pastoring a church just about an hour from Lebanon. Joe Varossa, one of the board members, and his wife Debra were asked to go to White House to hear me preach. I had no idea that they were coming. They were told, if they liked what they heard, to invite me to come minister at their church. After preaching two Sunday services, we were voted in as the pastors of Love's Way Community Church, receiving a 100 percent vote from the Board of Elders and the congregation. God proved Himself faithful as we simply stepped out in faith and began our new assignment with passion and expectancy. The church began to grow; more and more people came each week as the Lord gave the increase.

We quickly outgrew the small space where we were meeting. We started praying about moving to a larger facility to reach even more precious souls for the Kingdom. After looking at several building sites and properties, I felt impressed by the Lord to begin fasting and praying for seven days. I asked the elders of the church to join me. At the end of the seven days, the Lord opened a door for us to purchase the old Fairview Baptist Church in Lebanon, Tennessee, in 2015. Although the building was in desperate need of repair, many volunteers came and tirelessly worked. By removing old stained carpets, repairing and painting walls, and renovating bathrooms, we brought the old 27,000 square foot building back to life.

In the midst of this blessing, I received a supernatural warning from the Lord in a dream. I was standing in front of a large church building, of which I was the pastor. I knew that it was a Sunday service in progress, and I heard people singing. Something, however, felt strange and out of place as I looked in. I was not exactly sure what caused me to feel so unwelcome and disappointed at what I saw and heard. I remember turning around and slowly walking away. Suddenly I noticed a man walking beside me. It was Joe Varossa. He locked his arm in mine, and without saying a word, he just smiled and continued to walk with me.

It was several months later that the dream became clear, and I understood its meaning. Satan raised his ugly head and began attacking my family, my role as pastor, and everything we had worked so hard to accomplish for God. There were many sleepless nights and countless hours of prayer. I cried out to God for wisdom and strength on what to do and how to move forward. Timely words of encouragement would come from a brother or a sister who did not know anything about what we were going through. I also received supernatural reassurances from the Lord through dreams and visions.

During this time of trial, I had another dream. I was standing in an open field facing a raging bull. His shoulders were massive. Smoke was coming from his nostrils. The bull stomped his foot repeatedly, then lowered his head as if to charge. He was very angry. I specifically noticed his two large, sharp horns and realized what they could do to me. The bull began charging. I looked around for a place to hide, but there was nowhere to run. With my heart racing and the bull just a few feet away, I stood still and waited for the impact. Suddenly, the fierce bull disappeared in a puff of smoke. I remembered breathing a sigh of relief. I was not hurt; there was not one scratch on my body.

After I woke up, I knew the Lord was with me, and I had nothing to fear. He would be with my family and me, and we would not only accomplish what He had called us to do but see His hand do exceedingly abundantly more than what we could even imagine. We began to experience a strong presence of the Lord in every service. The praise and worship went to a completely new level. The worship team began to move in a prophetic flow that ushered us into the throne room of heaven. People would linger for hours at the altar, some on the floor face down, and others were standing with hands raised. The word was spoken with such freedom and authority. The enemy's plan failed. The Lord showed us once again, when we place everything in His hands, He will fight our battles. All we have to do is allow Holy Spirit to have complete control.

"No weapon formed against you will prevail,
and you will refute every tongue that accuses you.
This is the heritage of the servants of the Lord, and this is
their vindication from me, declares the Lord."
Isaiah 54:17 KJV

It has been years since the Lord revealed His faithfulness through these dreams and visions. We continue to experience an incredible move of the Holy Spirit in our services. People are lingering in His presence, from young to old, wanting more. Families are being restored; sons and daughters are returning home. People are coming to Jesus, discovering their identity and purpose. Hope and joy can be seen on their faces. It feels like the book of Acts is coming to life right before our eyes. Supernatural healings are taking place. There is a shift in the atmosphere.

29

KEEPERS OF THE VALLEY

The early church experienced rapid growth after the outpouring of the Holy Spirit. Signs, wonders, and miracles were wrought by the hands of the apostles. At the same time, the enemy wreaked havoc, trying everything to stop the move of God. Disciples were driven out of towns and villages, many martyred for the cause of Christ. Amid the persecution, from then until now, the church continues to advance.

From the moment John stepped onto the scene until now, the realm of heaven's kingdom is bursting forth, and passionate people have taken hold of its power.
Matthew 11:12 TPT

In 2020, the world was greatly affected by the Corona Virus outbreak, known as Covid-19. I believe this was orchestrated by hell itself, hurting people worldwide, and especially a direct attack on the Church of the Lord Jesus Christ. Prior to the pandemic or pan-demonic as I call it, the Lord gave me several warnings.

The warnings came in two dreams. I believe they were to help prepare us for what was to come. In the first dream, I saw satan standing at the head of a large table in what appeared to be an underground bunker. It reminded me of a military operation. Large demonic beings were plotting and planning attacks. The table was covered in papers, drawings, and maps. They were all standing, leaning over the table, discussing strategies, and giving specific orders to demonic spirits.

My attention was drawn to a large wall of shelves filled with trophies of all sizes. On the top shelf were large trophies, and I somehow knew these were awarded to demons who successfully defeated a Pastor, an Evangelist, a Bible Teacher, or anyone who preached the gospel. These large trophies were placed on the wall as a reminder of their victories. There were also trophies awarded for defeating intercessors, families, and marriages. I believe this dream was a call to fervently pray and also to lift the roof off and expose their evil plotting.

A few weeks later, I had another dream. I was standing in a wooded area, elevated on a large rock, overlooking a wide clearing. From my vantage point, I could see many people down in a valley. As I looked to my right, I saw several ferocious lions with their eyes fixed on the people. I knew they were in great danger, and I had to do something to

190

warn them. I needed to get them over a nearby fence to safety. As the lions started charging, I began running as fast as I could, shouting a warning. When I got to them, I immediately began lifting people and pushing them over the fence as fast as I could. Miraculously, everyone made it to safety. I believe that this was yet another warning of the Lord to be vigilant in prayer and to be alert. There is protection and safety in Him.

I shared these warnings with our congregation. We began to pray and intercede, cutting off the plots and plans of the enemy over our church family, city, and region.

I believe God was preparing us to fully trust Him and walk in His divine wisdom. By the time the demonic virus had devastated our nation and the world, we were learning to walk by faith and not be crippled or tormented by fear. Not to say that our congregation was not affected because we too felt the effects, but the Grace of God carried us through.

During this time, the Lord laid on my heart to have a tent revival in our city and confirmed it in several ways. As soon as we started planning, we heard of a Tent Revival in Texas. In July, Elize and I were able to attend. The man of God leading the event prayed over the pastors in attendance and encouraged us to take back our cities in the Name of Jesus. He declared we are the keepers of the valley. This was another confirmation of what the Lord had impressed upon us. We were in negotiations to purchase a piece of property, and the landowner was kind enough to allow us to hold a tent revival on this land.

We stepped out in faith and purchased a beautiful large white tent that could seat up to 1,000 people. Some questioned whether we should even do such a thing during a pandemic. However, as the news spread of the Lebanon Awakening Tent Revival, there was great excitement and expectancy.

In October of 2020, we set up the large tent. The sound of our worship could be heard from a distance. A man living in the woods heard the music and started walking toward it. Wearing a short-sleeved shirt that chilly night, he came into the tent. One of our volunteers saw him and gave him a jacket. When the invitation was given, he walked straight down the center aisle to the altar and gave his heart to Jesus! He then turned, left the tent, and simply walked back into the woods.

Night after night, we saw the hand of God move. Curious about what was going on, people driving by would often make a U-turn and come back. This happened one evening with a lady and her son while driving from Pennsylvania to Florida. She saw the billboard and big lights when she pulled off the interstate to get gas. To satisfy her curiosity, she drove to the tent. One of our team members, Jackie Snider, greeted her at her car and offered to walk her into the meeting. She refused and shared that she was in great physical pain. He asked if she believed Jesus could heal her. "Yes," she anxiously replied, "but don't tell my husband because if he finds out, he will get angry and leave me." He prayed for her while she sat in her car. Suddenly, she jumped out of her car and began running and shouting, "The Lord has touched me. I am healed!" Her thirteen-year-old son began crying, saying, "I haven't seen my mom feel this good in a long time." Still praising God, she got back in her car and drove away.

Each night, the tent was filled with people anticipating an encounter with The Holy Spirit. People from all walks of life, desperately needing a touch from God, filled the altars with tears streaming down their faces, surrendering their lives to the Lord. I saw those who were obviously familiar with tent revivals and the move of God, but some seemed to have absolutely no idea of what to expect. I saw those with hopelessness and brokenness in their eyes. As I stood and watched, I softly prayed, "Oh God, do a work in the lives of these precious people. Let them not leave without Your touch, without Your love reaching deep inside."

One man stood beside me and told me his story. He said he left home when he was very young, and today was his fiftieth birthday. He found himself living on the streets, sleeping under bridges, on park benches, and at friends' homes. He soon got into trouble with drugs and alcohol and spent time in prison. As I listened to his story, I began to feel great compassion for him. I wrapped my arms around him and assured him that God loved him and still had a purpose for his life.

That night, my son Andrew preached about the transforming power of the Holy Spirit. I remember watching the man and how intently he listened to every word throughout the whole service. My eyes filled with tears when he responded to the altar call. He walked straight to me and threw his arms around me. I began praying with him, and through a flood of tears, he surrendered his life to the Lord. Happy and overjoyed, he reached over to his friends and started hugging them. He had been forgiven and set free by the power of the Holy Spirit. This is what tent revival is all about!

When I looked over the many people who filled the altars that night, I could not help but think back on my father's ministry in South Africa. As compassion filled my heart, I understood what he felt when he looked at the throngs of people that came to Jesus in the tent crusades. I've watched as tears rolled down Dad's face when he would pray for the sick, the suffering, the poor, and those who were oppressed and possessed by the devil. Dad preached the glorious gospel of Jesus Christ for over thirty years in every village, town, and city in the beautiful country of South Africa.

Jesus Christ the same, yesterday, today, and forever.
Hebrew 13:8 (NKJV)

30

THE BIG GOSPEL TENT

Dad's passing still feels like it was yesterday. Even though the heartache is gone, it is impossible to forget the moment that changed my life forever. I can still hear the song that played in the background as we rolled his casket out of the Johannesburg Civic Center:

"I am going to a city,
Where the streets of gold are laid,
Where the tree of life is blooming,
I am going where the roses never fade."

It was a live recording of my dad singing that filled the auditorium that afternoon. Dad would often break out in song while preaching, and this was one of his favorites, Where the Roses Never Fade.

I remember thousands gathering at the gravesite. The sky was gray, and there was a gentle rain falling. People were softly singing as they lowered the casket. As we stood there holding hands, we made a vow to pick up the mantle and continue preaching the gospel.

People often ask if the family of the late Reverend George McGregor is still busy in ministry. It has been my joy to share with them that not only are they continuing, but by God's grace have expanded the ministry and are reaching more souls for the Kingdom. It has been a little more than thirty-six years since Dad went home to be with the Lord.

George and his wife Cecelia are still evangelizing nationwide and overseas. Known as the Elvis of South Africa, George continues to bless multitudes through his anointed worship.

Gershon, with the support of his wife Jeanne, continues to go where the doors are opened to spread the gospel, both in the U.S. and abroad.

Owen is the bishop and overseer of the many satellite churches that Dad started in South Africa. He and his wife Maggie are lead pastors of Mount Calvary Pentecostal Church, which is housed in a two thousand five hundred seat tent in Johannesburg.

Rosalind and her husband Dan are generous supporters of all the brothers and their ministries, undergirding them with fervent prayer.

Greg and his wife Marie continue to minister the gospel of Jesus Christ, preaching in revivals and conferences.

Manuel and his wife Joeline evangelized for many years and are now the pastors of Harvest Church of Murfreesboro, Tennessee.

Roy, with the support of his wife Bernadette, is the associate pastor and worship leader of The River in Portland, Tennessee.

Dad's gravesite is located in a beautiful, serene park in Johannesburg, South Africa. Because of his love and passion for tent revivals, we had his gravestone carved into the shape of a Big Gospel Tent.

What a beautiful symbol a tent has become in my life. It is more than just vinyl, ropes, and metal poles. To me, it represents reaching precious souls for the Kingdom of God. It also speaks of a family called by God to fulfill His purpose in their generation; a father, a mother, and eight children ministering the gospel of Jesus Christ for more than 30 years in South Africa. Watching Dad preach, Mom interceding, my siblings leading worship, and seeing the miraculous happen will forever be in my heart.

I'm reminded of the scripture, *"Enlarge the place of your tent, stretch your tent curtains wide, do not hold back; lengthen your cords, strengthen your stakes."*
Isaiah 54:2 (NIV)

I see this scripture unfolding in my own life as Elize and I are together on this journey of faith, along with our children. Even when they were very young, we dedicated them to the Lord, just as my father and mother had dedicated us. We are so grateful to the Lord for our beautiful children, who love God with all their hearts and to see them active in the Kingdom. They are standing with us in ministry, ready to serve in any capacity. Andrew and Kimi, their children (Gabriella, Ezra, Judah, and Elisha Wesley); Raymond; Brandon and Emily with their children (Levi and Shia); Chantelle and Tim with their son, (Jeremiah); Justin and Jonathan, our twin boys, are all active in ministry. Now, to see our amazing grandchildren serving the Lord is priceless! I believe that God has a very specific call on each of their lives, and our greatest joy is to see them fulfilling it.

In May 2018, my dear friends in Holland, Pastor David Maasbach and Evangelist, John T.L. Maasbach, asked me to hold a soul-winning and healing crusade in DRC - The Republic of Congo.

Raymond, was doing missionary work in the neighboring country of Uganda and joined me in DRC a few days later. We were warmly received by Apostle Tambu Lukoli and started a week-long crusade in the city of Kinshasa. It was open-air meetings. The streets were blocked off, so the crowds of people could sit or stand on the roads. We were set up on a high stage, at an intersection where four roads met, and people were all around us.

Thousands came to the meetings every night, expecting to receive from the hand of God. We saw hundreds upon hundreds surrender their lives to Jesus night after night. A tangible presence of the Holy Spirit was present, and many received miraculous healings and the baptism of the Holy Spirit.

I remember one night, while I was preaching, my voice gave out. I motioned Raymond to come and take over. He came and continued the message under the anointing. What a mighty God we serve!

I feel very blessed that God called my children into ministry, and that they heeded the call!

Currently, our children are serving with us at Love's Way Church: Andrew is the executive associate pastor and worship leader. His wife, Kimi, is the children's church director. Raymond is a worship leader, children's church teacher, young adult leader, and missionary. Brandon is the worship band leader, accomplished musician, and singer/songwriter. His wife Emily serves in the visual/creative arts department and nursery. Chantelle is the youth pastor and a worship leader. Her husband, Tim, is the lead audio/visual technical engineer. Justin is on-site at Austin Peay University campus ministry and worship leader. Jonathan is a worship leader, creative social media designer, and photographer.

God has surely enlarged the place of the McGregor tent!

Children are God's love-gift; they are heaven's generous reward. Children born to a young couple will one day rise to protect and provide for their parents.
Happy will be the couple who has many of them! A household full of children will not bring shame on your name but victory when you face your enemies for your offspring will have influence and honor to prevail on your behalf!
Psalm 127:3-5 (TPT)

Even in our church, God continues to expand His ministry. The Lord gave me a vision in 2020, which I shared with our church family. The vision included property to accommodate our growing congregation, a large worship center, a beautiful children's church area, ample space for our growing student ministry, an International Bible Training Center, and a 24-Hour Prayer Room. In early 2021, we stepped out in faith and bought twenty-one beautiful acres on Hwy 231 South, at 1315 Murfreesboro Road, Lebanon, Tennessee.

My Beautiful Family:

Brandon, Emily, Levi, (Shia - not pictured);

Andrew, Kimi, Gabriella, Ezra, Judah,

(Elisha Wesley - not pictured);

Tim, Chantelle, Jeremiah;

Raymond, Jonathan, Justin,

Johan and Elize

Epilogue

The true legacy a man leaves behind is best seen in the deeds of his sons. What a wonderful legacy George and Mary McGregor left behind. What a wonderful testimony to the faithfulness of God.

We know beyond a shadow of a doubt that God called us as missionaries from Africa to America. Even though the road was paved with many hardships and disappointments, we hold no grudges or ill feelings towards anyone. We realize that if everything worked out perfectly in Austin, Texas, we would have never made it to Lincolnton, North Carolina. And if they had not canceled the revivals and offered us no assistance, we would still be there. I believe that God had something far greater planned for us in Tennessee through a Happy pastor, Paul Baggett. Yes, it was the providence of Almighty God that brought us thus far by faith.

As we see the Kingdom of God rapidly advancing, we are sitting on the edge of our seats; wondering what God will do next!

What a time to be alive.